Understanding the Reggio Approach

Understanding the Reggio Approach is a much needed source of information for those wishing to extend and consolidate their understanding of the Reggio Approach. It enables analysis of the essential elements of this particular approach to early childhood teaching and the relationship it holds with quality early years practice.

It describes the key features of the Reggio Approach to early childhood including the environment, creativity, relationships and documentation. This new edition has been updated with the latest developments in this approach and includes new material on the thinking and work of Loris Malaguzzi and the future for educators in Reggio Emilia and the implications for practice in the UK. Features include:

- examples from infant–toddler centres and preschools in Reggio Emilia;
- key points to highlight the ideas that practitioners should consider when reviewing and reflecting on their practice;
- reflections that can be used as the basis for continuing professional development and action research.

Written to support the work of all those in the field of early education and childcare, this is a vital text for students, early years and childcare practitioners, teachers, early years professionals, children's centre professionals, lecturers, advisory teachers and setting managers.

Linda Thornton has extensive experience in the field of education and childcare. She has provided consultancy and training for local authorities, children's centres, nurseries and schools across the UK.

Pat Brunton has provided training and consultancy for local authorities, children's centres, nurseries and schools across the UK.

Understanding the... Approach
Series Editors: Pat Brunton and Linda Thornton

This new series provides a much needed source of information for those wishing to extend and consolidate their understanding of international approaches to early years education and childcare. The books will enable the reader to analyse the essential elements of each approach and its relationship to quality early years practice.

Each book:

- describes the key principles of the approach to early childhood with practical examples and case studies;
- provides students and practitioners with the relevant information about a key pedagogical influence on high quality early years practice;
- highlights the key ideas that practitioners should consider when reviewing and reflecting on their own practice;
- can be used as the basis for continuing professional development and action research.

Written to support the work of all those in the field of early years education and childcare, these will be invaluable texts for students, early years and childcare practitioners, teachers, early years professionals, children's centre professionals, lecturers, advisory teachers, head teachers and setting managers.

Understanding the Reggio Approach

Early years education
in practice

Third Edition

Linda Thornton and Pat Brunton

 Routledge
Taylor & Francis Group

LONDON AND NEW YORK

Third edition published 2015
by Routledge
2 Park Square, Milton Park, Abingdon, Oxon OX14 4RN

and by Routledge
711 Third Avenue, New York, NY 10017

Routledge is an imprint of the Taylor & Francis Group, an informa business

First edition published by David Fulton Publishers 2005
Second edition published by Routledge/David Fulton 2009

British Library Cataloguing in Publication Data
A catalogue record for this book is available from the British Library

Library of Congress Cataloging-in-Publication Data
A catalog record for this book has been requested

ISBN: 978-1-138-78437-6 (hbk)
ISBN: 978-1-138-78438-3 (pbk)
ISBN: 978-1-315-74401-8 (ebk)

Typeset in Palatino
by Sunrise Setting Ltd, Paignton, UK

*The views expressed in this publication are those of the authors representing
their own interpretation of the philosophy and practices of the municipal
infant–toddler centres and preschools of Reggio Emilia.*

*The content of this publication has not been officially approved by the
Municipality of Reggio Emilia nor by Reggio Children in Italy; therefore
it may not reflect the views and opinions of these organisations.*

Contents

Contents

Introduction

It's our country that's shaped like a boot. The country is Italy. It's bigger than the cities and inside it there are all the cities. There are probably three billion cities![1]

No-one in Reggio wants to teach others how to 'do school'. What we want to do rather is to try and deepen our understanding, together with others, of why it was possible in Reggio Emilia for an (educational) experience founded after the war, to grow and consolidate with time . . . . . What we want to do is to look together for the values we might have in common, in order to build a better tomorrow.

(Amelia Gambetti, Executive
Coordinator of the Reggio Children organisation 1998)

An increasing number of people in the UK have been touched by the 'Reggio experience' in some way – through visiting Reggio Emilia on a study tour, viewing *The Hundred Languages of Children* exhibition or being involved in one of the many projects across the country which draw their inspiration from the work of the Reggio preschools and infant–toddler centres. We have visited Reggio Emilia on five occasions since 1999. In 1999/2000 we were involved in the arrangements for the 2000 visit of *The Hundred Languages of Children* exhibition to the UK, hosted a visit for educators from Reggio, and initiated an arts and early years research project and exhibition. Since then we have maintained our links with educators in Reggio and have worked collaboratively to help disseminate a wider understanding of the Reggio Emilia Approach to education.

Since 2001, at seminars and presentations we have given across the country, the comments made, and the questions posed, have been very similar. Participants have been inspired and excited by their introduction to the Reggio Approach, and are keen to find out more. Many beautifully illustrated books have been produced by the Reggio Children organisation describing the work of the infant–toddler centres and preschools and the philosophy behind the Reggio Approach (see the Appendix). There are also several publications from educators in Australia, the USA and the rest of Europe describing their response to the Reggio experience (Cadwell 1997, 2003; Gedin 1998; Abbott and Nutbrown 2001; Millikan 2003; Wurm 2005; Lewin-Benham 2006, 2008).

The aim of this book is to share our understanding of the research-based approach to early education of Reggio Emilia. It is subjective, in that it represents our personal interpretation of what we have seen and heard in Reggio Emilia, based on our visits, discussions with 'pedagogistas', 'atelieristas' and teachers, and supported by extensive research, reflection and discussion. As succinctly put by Carlina Rinaldi, pedagogical consultant to Reggio Children, 'You can only see what you know'. When we first visited the preschools in 1999 we saw science and technology, not art, and experienced children as researchers, not artists. The truth is they are both. 'Each child is an artist, each child a scientist' (Bruner 2004).

Wherever possible we have provided references to original sources from Reggio to substantiate our interpretations. We encourage you to read (and reread) these texts to further your own understanding of the Reggio Approach, and then to consider how it can be used as a source of inspiration for your work with young children.

Background to the UK interest in the Reggio Approach

Interest in the Reggio Approach began in the mid-1980s when educators from Reggio first visited the UK, and blossomed during the early 1990s here, as well as in the rest of the world, following the article in *Newsweek* magazine in 1991 naming the Diana School as the best early childhood institution in the world. During the 1990s, some early exchange visits took place between educators, administrators and parents from Pen Green in Northamptonshire and Reggio Emilia (Ghedini *et al.* undated). In 1995, the Sightlines Initiative, based in Newcastle upon Tyne, was established, and by 1997 *The Hundred Languages of Children* exhibition made its first visit to the UK – to London and Newcastle – organised by Sightlines and the British Association for Early Childhood Education (BAECE) (now Early Education) (Gura 1997).

During 1997–8, early years practitioners and artists from the northeast of England attended the Summer and Winter Institutes, followed in subsequent years by a series of UK study tours organised through the Sightlines Initiative, and international study tours involving early years educators, artists, administrators, advisers, architects and academics from around the world.

In 2000, the *Hundred Languages* exhibition made a return visit to the UK where it spent a year visiting Cardiff, Belfast, Exeter, Bristol, Glasgow, Bradford and Coventry. During 2004, the *Hundred Languages* exhibition again visited the UK, with venues in Manchester, Newcastle, Cambridge, Kent and Birmingham. Extensive professional development programmes were run in association with both these exhibition visits, and projects drawing their inspiration from the work of Reggio have been developed in various parts of the country.

The study of the Reggio Emilia Approach to early education has, in recent years, been included in many graduate and postgraduate courses in UK universities and colleges, leading to a greater understanding of this important early years pedagogy.

The Early Years Foundation Stage (EYFS), introduced in England in 2008 (Department for Children, Schools and Families 2008), drew much of its inspiration from the Reggio Approach with its key principles – 'A Unique Child', 'Positive Relationships', 'Enabling Environments', 'Learning and Development' – reflecting the growing interest in the quality provision of Reggio Emilia encountered by UK practitioners. These guiding principles survived in the revised streamlined version of the EYFS introduced in 2012 (Department for Education 2012).

The structure of the book

Chapter 1 describes the context in which the philosophy and pedagogy of the early childhood institutions of Reggio Emilia developed. There is a focus on the life and influence of Loris Malaguzzi, the pedagogical founder of the Reggio Approach. The key aspects of the Reggio Approach are introduced, which will then be developed in more detail in later chapters. Although each chapter focuses on one aspect of the Reggio Approach, it will be evident that they are all interrelated and none can be considered in isolation.

Chapter 2 explains how the municipal infant–toddler centres and preschools fit into the overall organisation of early childhood services in the city of Reggio Emilia. Factual information on the organisation and running of the early childhood centre is provided and the different roles of the teacher, the pedagogista and the atelierista are described.

Chapters 3, 4 and 5 deal in more detail with space, relationships and time, respectively. These three aspects of the Reggio Approach are interdependent and closely related; changes in the management of any one aspect necessarily impact on the other two. Wherever possible, examples drawn from visits, seminars and talks have been included to illustrate the points being discussed.

Chapter 3 describes the design features and layout of the buildings and how these are incorporated into the spaces of a preschool or infant–toddler centre. Examples are given of how these spaces are inhabited during the course of the day.

Chapter 4 reviews the concept of reciprocal relationships – between people, with the environment and resources, and with the community. These are the relationships that underpin all the other aspects of the Reggio Approach.

Chapter 5 examines the use of time, in the short, medium and long term, and reviews the way learning opportunities are identified in day-to-day experiences and long-term projects.

Chapter 6 looks at the centrality of research in the ongoing educational experience in Reggio and develops the theme of the confident, competent child. Group organisation and group learning, significant features of the Reggio Approach, are discussed in more detail.

Chapter 7 considers the central role which creativity plays in the Reggio philosophy. It looks at the nature of creativity, how children's creativity and critical thinking are supported through the role of the adult and by the organisation of space, time and resources.

Chapter 8 describes the way in which documentation is used to visualise children's learning on a day-to-day basis. The tools of documentation are described and examples provided of documentation with babies, toddlers and young children.

Finally, Chapter 9 summarises what we feel are the key messages we can gain from understanding the work of the preschools and infant–toddler centres of Reggio Emilia.

The structure of the chapters

At the beginning of each chapter there is a brief summary of the content, followed by a more detailed description of the aspect under consideration. References to key texts are included to encourage the reader to extend their own research and understanding of the Reggio Approach. Chapters 1 to 8 are summarised in a set of ten 'Key Points', and there is a section in each of these chapters entitled 'Reflections on the Reggio Approach'. It is offered as a starting point, not a comprehensive list. It reflects many of the questions we have been asked by educators involved in planning professional development initiatives for themselves and their colleagues, and is primarily designed to be used as a group exercise, to highlight issues you may wish to consider as a team when reflecting on your practice.

The emphasis on collegiality and group involvement reflects our belief in the importance of shared input and shared responsibility in defining and implementing change.

The section at the end of Chapter 1 deals with 'the big issues'. We urge you to consider these first to help create your own vision for the future.

In the words of Jerome Bruner, 'Reggio is not a blueprint. It is an inspiration to be yourself and to find your own excellence and to perfect it' Bruner (2000: 123).

Acknowledgements

Writing the original version of this book was, and preparing this new edition has been, a challenging and thought-provoking experience, the culmination of many hours of research, reflection and reliving our personal Reggio experiences. We wish to thank friends and colleagues in Reggio Emilia and in the UK for their encouragement, interest and support in this process.

Note

1. *Reggio Tutta: A Guide to the City by the Children* © Municipality of Reggio Emilia – Infant–Toddler Centres and Preschools, published by Reggio Children 2000, p. 25.

References

Abbott, L. and Nutbrown, C. (eds) (2001) *Experiencing Reggio Emilia*, Open University Press, Buckingham, UK.

Bruner, J. (2000) 'Citizens of the world', in Davoli, M. and Ferri, G. (eds) *Reggio Tutta: A Guide to the City by the Children*, Reggio Children, Reggio Emilia, pp. 122–3.

Bruner, J. (2004) Video-conference address at Crossing Boundaries International Conference, February, Reggio Emilia.

Cadwell, L. B. (1997) *Bringing Reggio Emilia Home*, Teachers College Press, Columbia University, New York and London.

Cadwell, L. B. (2003) *Bringing Learning to Life. The Reggio Approach to Early Childhood Education*, Teachers College Press, Columbia University, New York and London.

Department for Children, Schools and Families (2008) *The Early Years Foundation Stage: Setting the Standards for Learning, Development and Care for Children from Birth to Five*, Department for Children, Schools and Families. Available online at http://nsonline.org.uk/node/157774?uc=force_uj (last accessed September 2014).

Department for Education (2012) *Statutory Framework for the Early Years Foundation Stage: Setting the Standards for Learning, Development and Care for Children from Birth to Five*, Department for Education. Available online at www.gov.uk/government/publications/early-years-foundation-stage-framework (last accessed September 2014).

Gambetti, A. (1998) 'The Winter Institute: An International Meeting on Education', *rechild*, 2, Reggio Children, Reggio Emilia.

Gedin, M. (ed.) (1998) 'Discovering the inquisitive child', *Modern Childhood*, 6, Reggio Emilia Institute, Stockholm.

Ghedini, P. O., Chandler, T., Whalley, M. and Moss, P. (eds) (undated) *Fathers, Nurseries and Childcare*, Report from European Commission Network on Childcare.

Gura, P. (ed.) (1997) *Reflections on Early Education and Care*, Early Education, London.

Lewin-Benham, A. (2006) *Possible Schools – The Reggio Approach to Urban Education*, Teachers College Press, Columbia University, New York and London.

Lewin-Benham, A. (2008) *Powerful Children – Understanding How to Teach and Learn Using the Reggio Approach*, Teachers College Press, Columbia University, New York and London.

Millikan, J. (2003) *Reflections: Reggio Emilia Principles within Australian Contexts*, Pademelon Press, New South Wales.

Wurm, J. P. (2005) *Working in the Reggio Way*, Redleaf Press, St Paul, MN.

1 The Reggio Emilia Approach to education, and Loris Malaguzzi

In Reggio everybody has a bike; the men, the mothers, the children . . . the grandparents, but they're the ones that are really used to it because they've been riding bikes for a long long time.[1]

Reggio successfully challenges so many false dichotomies: arts versus science, individual versus community, child versus adult, enjoyment versus study, nuclear family versus extended family. It does this by achieving a unique harmony that spans these contrasts.

(Gardner 1998: xvii)

This chapter looks at the geographical, historical, social and cultural influences that have shaped the philosophy and pedagogy of the pre-schools and infant–toddler centres of Reggio Emilia. The key features of the Reggio Approach and the influence of its founding pedagogue, Loris Malaguzzi – the image of the child, the concept of the hundred languages of expression, the role of the atelier, the use of documentation in group learning, the value placed upon space, time and relationships – are outlined. Each of these themes is developed in more detail in subsequent chapters.

Geography

Reggio Emilia is a small city in the Emilia Romagna region of Northern Italy, approximately 40 miles north-west of Bologna. It is a largely prosperous area supporting a diverse range of manufacturing business and light industry, and has been a flourishing commercial centre since it was founded in Roman times. Reggio is a modern, dynamic city which combines economic prosperity with social and ecological responsibility. It prides itself on being outward-looking and forward-thinking and has traditionally cooperated well with neighbouring cities.

To the visitor, Reggio is an attractive, well-organised and welcoming city which is famous for Parmigiano Reggiano (Parmesan) cheese, balsamic vinegar, Lambrusco wine and Max Mara clothing. There are interesting and beautiful churches, municipal buildings and theatres as well as fountains, gardens and public spaces. Life in the city centre revolves around the many piazzas and elegant boulevards that are particularly vibrant in the early evening and on market days.

The population, currently around 155,000, has risen by over 25,000 inhabitants since 1991. This is a consequence of a very high birth rate combined with immigration into the area from Southern Italy and from countries external to the European Union. Until 1996, the birth rate in Reggio Emilia was one of the lowest in Northern Italy. Consequently there are proportionally very few (16 per cent) young people under 18 years of age, in comparison to the number over 60 years of age (26 per cent). Immigrants constitute 6 per cent of the population, and are mostly between 25 and 39 years of age: their children make up 10 per cent of the under-5 years age group (Piccinini 2004, 2006).

In the beginning

When reading about the history of Italy it is clear that Reggio Emilia has long had a distinct identity and independence of thought and action. In January 1797 the red, white and green Tricolore, the flag adopted by the Cispadana Republic (the cities of Ferrara, Bologna, Modena and Reggio Emilia), which later became the Italian flag, first appeared in the Salon di Tricolore in Reggio.

From the early part of the twentieth century, the area of Emilia Romagna has, contrary to the rest of Italy, embraced 'enlightened communism'. During the Second World War, the area was devastated by Fascist and Nazi action because of its resistance to dictatorship and German occupation, and suffered considerable structural damage as a result of Allied bombing. In 1945, during the aftermath of war, the people urgently needed to rebuild their lives – not only materially but also socially and morally. They set about rebuilding homes and public buildings, developing cooperative movements to provide services, and redressing inequalities in their society. Throughout this period, the women of the area were the powerful force behind the development of early childhood services.

The municipal preschools of Reggio Emilia came into existence in 1963, but their origins lie in the period immediately following Liberation Day in 1945. In the village of Villa Cella, seven kilometres from Reggio, a small amount of money was made available to the community by the Committee of National Liberation. This money came from the sale of a tank, a few horses and a truck that had been abandoned by the retreating Nazis. The men of the village suggested building a theatre; the women wanted to build a preschool to provide a new form of education that would ensure that they would never again bring up a generation of children who would tolerate injustice and inequality.

Through negotiation and debate, it was agreed that the preschool would be built. A local farmer contributed the land, a building cooperative gave the services of its construction engineer and machinery, and the local population – men and women of all ages – provided the labour. The building materials came from the bombed-out buildings of the village and the surrounding area.

Loris Malaguzzi (1920–94)

In 1945, Loris Malaguzzi, the inspiration behind the educational experience in Reggio Emilia, was an elementary school teacher in Reggio when he first heard rumours of the project taking place in Villa Cella. He cycled out to the village to see if what he had heard was true.

> I went home. My feelings of wonder, and the sense of the extraordinary, were stronger than my happiness . . . . All of my little models were laughingly over-turned; that building a school would ever occur to the people, women, farm la-bourers, factory workers, farmers was in itself traumatic. But that these same peo-ple, without a penny to their names, with no technical offices, building permits, site directors, inspectors from the Ministry of Education or the Party, could actually build a school with their own strength, brick by brick, was the second paradox.
>
> (Malaguzzi 2000: 13)

Loris Malaguzzi was born in Correggio on the 23 February 1920 where he lived under Fascist rule from the age of two. He was encouraged by his father to enrol on a teacher training course in 1939, graduating with a degree in Pedagogy from the University of Urbino where he studied during the Second World War. He then went to Rome in 1946 to attend one of the first post-war child psychology courses, achieving a degree from the Italian National Research Centre (CNR). While in Rome, he worked as a child psychologist and educator.

Malaguzzi remembered 6 years of war that 'gobbled up my youth' (Fixquotes 2014) and was determined that he would build a better future for the children and families of Reggio Emilia. Malaguzzi told the story of the beginnings of the Reggio Emilia Approach to education and how he was determined from the outset to try to change the lives and fulfil the aspirations of those families greatly affected by war and the political leadership of their country:

> These women were cleaning bricks near the river, so I asked them what they were doing. 'We're making a school' they answered, and that's how it all got started. The women asked me to look after their children. 'Our children are just as intelligent as the rich people's children,' they said proudly, asking me to teach their children enough to give them a better chance in life. I told them that I had no experience, but promised to do my best. 'I'll learn as we go along and the children will learn everything I learn working with them'.
>
> (Achtner 1994)

Malaguzzi wanted the infant–toddler centres and preschools to help develop children who would be happy to look back on their rich child-hood. He brought to his lifetime's work in education his many interests and experiences in the theatre, journalism, sport and politics. Susanna

Mantovani, professor at the University of Milan-Bicocca, saw Malaguzzi as a man with intellectual curiosity, with the eye of the artist, a man of the theatre whose theories became refined without losing sight of his politics (Mantovani 2004). He is remembered by his colleagues as a very strong character, but highly collaborative, paying attention to each individual but a constant weaver of networks (Mantovani 2004), and Malaguzzi described himself thus:

> I am very tenacious, very stubborn, an iron will. I never want to lose a battle. I want to win and I have to carry along with me everyone who thinks like me, or thinks better than me, or even differently from me.
>
> (Barsotti 2004: 15)

In Malaguzzi's obituary in *The Independent* newspaper Wolfgang Achtner says:

> Loris Malaguzzi was greatly respected and even venerated by all who worked with him. He embodied the best of Italian virtues: commitment, creativity and that uncanny ingenuity that permits his countrymen to make do in any situation, even with the least of materials.
>
> (Achtner 1994)

One of Malaguzzi's closest colleagues, Carlina Rinaldi says:

> Malaguzzi never concealed the great expectations and hopes he had for the teachers. Those who knew him remember very well how he could also be exacting and demanding (though first of all with himself). But we also know that this was a tangible sign of the deep respect and gratitude he felt for teachers: respect for their intelligence, abilities and possibilities.
>
> (Rinaldi 2006: 59)

At the Crossing Boundaries International Conference held in Reggio Emilia in 2004, to celebrate the life and work of Loris Malaguzzi 10 years after his death, Carlina Rinaldi made a moving tribute to Loris Malaguzzi, the man, when she said he was 'a lovely leader due to his ability to promote a sense of belongingness, to cross borders, build hopes in dialogue with challenges and joys. Malaguzzi loved to live on borders where people can meet and knowledge develop' (Rinaldi 2004).

Until his sudden death in 1994, 6 weeks after the death of his wife Nilde Bonaccini, Malaguzzi worked tirelessly with colleagues in Reggio, and further afield, to further his understanding of how children learn and to disseminate his passionate belief in his image of the competent, confident child. During his lifetime his work received universal academic recognition across much of the world, but his achievements received little widespread public acclaim either in Italy or abroad until the last 10 years of his life. It was after his death that the widespread international acclaim and recognition of the Reggio Approach to early education spread across the world. Carlina Rinaldi put into words the strong message that emanates from all those involved in early education in Reggio Emilia: 'This is to say that . . . the right to hope, and the right to the future, must always be the right of children and of adults; rights that all of us, the friends of Loris, are committed to defending together' (Rinaldi 2006: 60).

History

At the end of the Second World War, similar early childhood projects were developing in several of the poorest areas of Reggio Emilia, all created and run by parents. There was a strong sense of hope for the future arising from the adversity of the past.

For almost the next 20 years the preschools were reliant on the goodwill and support of their local communities for money, resources, food and skills. By the early 1960s the community-run system was becoming unsustainable, and in 1962 the Union of Italian Women, which ran many of the early preschools, called a regional conference in Reggio Emilia to highlight the need for quality services in both the country and the city.

Prior to the 1960s, preschools in Reggio, as in the rest of Italy, were the responsibility of the Roman Catholic Church. By now the system could no longer cope with the demand for places, and parents began to demand the right to send their children to secular schools. In 1963, the Municipality of Reggio Emilia began the setting up of a network of educational services that included the opening of the first preschools for children aged from 3 to 6 years. This was an important landmark. For the first time in Italy people affirmed their right to establish a secular school for young children. In the same year, it was suggested to the Municipality that it should take on responsibility for those preschools which had been established since 1945.

At the opening of the Loris Malaguzzi Centre in 2006, Renzo Bonazzi, mayor of Reggio Emilia from 1962 to 1976, recalled the 1960s and 1970s as tumultuous times as the Municipality tried to adapt to the changes in society with the proliferation of new workplaces and more women entering the workforce. The Municipality had to fight against the national laws to provide the schools they wanted, but there were conflicts at a local level which was dominated by the communist and socialist parties and the right wing national government. The Municipality received both political support and the support of women in raising the funds they needed to build the schools they wanted. Bonazzi explained that at the time Malaguzzi was not universally recognised as the appropriately skilled person to lead the new schools but he, the mayor, was convinced he was the right choice. Those who supported him saw the preschools not as warehouses for children, but rather they wanted to create places where they would develop their own personalities and not simply obey. They knew they needed to provide teachers who shared this vision for early education. Bonazzi wanted to see fewer schools but of high quality: this was not even popular with his own political party as they were seen as too expensive (Bonazzi 2006).

Following protracted negotiations the early preschools became part of the municipal network between 1967 and 1973 (Barazzoni 2000).

Loris Malaguzzi recalls this period in the development of the preschools as the stage when the schools recognised the need to engage with the community of Reggio Emilia to win their trust and respect.

> Once a week we would transport the school to town. Literally, we would pack ourselves, the children, and our tools into a truck and we would teach school and show exhibits in the open air, in public parks or under the colonnade of the municipal theatre. The children were happy. The people saw; they were surprised and they asked questions.
>
> (Malaguzzi 1998: 52)

In 1970, the first infant–toddler centre, for children aged 3 months to 3 years, was opened by the Municipality in response to the demands of working mothers. To overcome the resistance of the church, and the fear that this would lead to the breakdown of family structures, the centres were described as providers of early childhood education in environments that were appropriate to the children's developmental level.

Political opposition to the existence of the Municipal Preschools of Reggio Emilia, and all that they stood for, lasted until 1976 when Gustavo Selva, a national radio commentator, launched a 7-day offensive against the early childhood policies of the Municipality. In answer to this attack, the preschools were opened up to public scrutiny and debate for a period of several months. The parents and the community confirmed their support for the guiding principles of the Reggio Approach to early childhood education, creating the strong reciprocal relationship between the preschools and the community that exists today.

During the 1980s, the network of preschools and infant–toddler centres increased in number to 21 preschools and 13 infant–toddler centres, catering for 50 per cent of 3- to 6-year-olds and 30 per cent of babies and toddlers in the area (Reggio Children 1999). By 2004 this had increased to 22 preschools and 24 infant–toddler centres. In 2008 the Nidi Julia Maramotti (an infant–toddler centre) was opened, funded jointly by the Municipality and the Max Mara Foundation, and the original preschool in the village of Sesso was replaced in a joint venture with a local entrepreneur. The number of preschools and infant–toddler centres operating as affiliated cooperatives continues to grow and there is now close collaboration between municipal, state and private preschools to plan new places, provide information for parents and provide professional development opportunities for teachers. Between them, the preschools and infant–toddler centres in Reggio Emilia provide places for more than 4,000 children, satisfying the demand from parents.

The organisation of the preschools and infant–toddler centres is looked at in detail in Chapter 2.

International interest

In 1980, a national early education research group was established in Reggio, the Gruppo Nazionale Nidi e Infanzia, and in the same year an exhibition of the work of the preschools and infant–toddler centres *When the Eye Jumps Over the Wall* was shown in the city for the first time. This exhibition travelled to Stockholm the following year triggering what was to become a growing international interest in learning more about the Reggio Approach. By 1987, the exhibition had been redesigned and duplicated to become *The Hundred Languages of Children* exhibition, which has visited many countries throughout the world (Filippini and Vecchi 1997: 19).

The first international interest in the Reggio experience came from Sweden in 1979, followed by delegations of visitors from Cuba, Bulgaria, Spain, Japan, Switzerland and France. In 1991, the American magazine, *Newsweek*, named the Diana preschool as the most avant-garde early childhood institution in the world, leading to huge interest from the

USA and the rest of the world. By 1994, national and international interest in the work of the preschools had increased to such an extent that a public company, Reggio Children, was established to manage the international study tours and numerous requests from educationalists around the world.

The name 'Reggio Children' had only just been decided upon when, tragically, Loris Malaguzzi died unexpectedly. The community of Reggio Emilia resolved to carry on and implement his dreams and fulfil the Reggio Children mission 'to enhance the potential of all children'. Ten years on, in February 2004, 'Crossing Boundaries', an international conference, with 1,500 delegates from 52 countries, was held to celebrate the life of Malaguzzi and the fortieth anniversary of the first municipal preschool.

Between 1994 and 2006, 130 study groups, with 16,200 participants from 90 different countries, were organised by Reggio Children. In July 2006 the first meeting of the Reggio Children International Network was held, with representatives from 14 countries, to promote international dialogue about children and childhood. Since the opening of the Malaguzzi Centre in 2006, more than 4,000 participants a year from Italy and 110 other countries have taken part in study groups in Reggio Emilia. International conferences are held in countries across the world, there are opportunities to visit the Malaguzzi Centre as individuals or guided small groups, and workshops for companies and professionals can be arranged. There are also limited opportunities to study on a master's programme or to attend a longer professional development course.

Social and cultural context

The way in which the Reggio philosophy has developed has inevitably been shaped by the social and cultural influences of the area. Emilia Romagna has a long tradition of democratic involvement, collegiality, participation and responsible citizenship. In their daily lives, the people of Reggio Emilia value encounters, discussion, debate and negotiation. Human relationships are important at both individual and civic levels, and different opinions, viewpoints and cultures are welcomed. Immigration throughout the 1980s and 1990s has resulted in a wide cultural mix involving more than a hundred different ethnic groups. At the local administrative level, the Municipality of Reggio Emilia is responding positively to these changes with the educational system seen as the key to defining and developing a new multi-ethnic future (Borghi 2004).

Influences

Right from the beginning, educators in Reggio have been interested in gathering ideas and opinions from as wide a range of sources as possible. In developing their approach in the 1960s, they actively sought information from existing pedagogical structures and philosophies all over the world. Theories of and experience in the sociology, psychology and philosophy of education, including the work of Montessori, Piaget, Dewey, Vygotsky, Isaacs, Freire, Bronfenbrenner, Bruner and Gardner were analysed, discussed and incorporated where appropriate. In addition, the ideas and works of artists, scientists, philosophers, writers, poets, historians, anthropologists and linguists have been drawn upon to create a rich pool of intellectual thought and action (Hoyuelos 2004: 8). Particularly significant during the 1960s and 1970s were the opportunities to meet and debate with the educationalist Bruno Ciari and the writer Gianni Rodari (Filippini and Vecchi 1997: 19). The names given to many of the preschools and infant–toddler centres acknowledge the very outward-looking, eclectic nature of their educational influences and are a fascinating route map through European intellectual thought.

During the 1960s, the views and opinions of the local community were sought by taking the schools out weekly to inhabit the piazzas of the city, and conferences and seminars were organised with educationalists from the rest of Italy. This enthusiasm for the exchange of ideas has grown over the years, through *The Hundred Languages of Children* exhibition, international study tours, the publications of Reggio Children, and collaborative research projects.

In the words of Loris Malaguzzi: 'Our whole history has been graced in different ways with important people. It has been our great fortune to find them, to have encountered them walking along the same road, above all to have known them in person (Barsotti 2004: 13).

The Reggio philosophy

Research into children's thinking and learning plays a critical role in determining how the philosophy and pedagogy in Reggio develops. When talking about their philosophy, educators describe their approach as a long-term educational research project where children and adults are learning alongside one another – building the present, not forgetting the past, and looking to the future. They recognise the importance of understanding more about how children learn, and consider every child as a gifted child who needs a gifted teacher. Children with disabilities are fully integrated into the structure and are spoken of as 'children with special rights' (Smith 1998). In Reggio there is no predetermined curriculum. Children's learning is developed through their involvement in long- and short-term projects which develop out of first-hand experiences and their theories about the world.

The image of the child

Fundamental to the Reggio Approach is the image of the child as rich in potential, strong, powerful and competent. At the centre of the Reggio pedagogy is the child who is confident in building relationships, who holds his or her own values, who wants to be respected and valued for himself as well as holding a respect for others, and who embodies a curiosity and open-mindedness to all that is possible.

Children are encouraged to develop their own theories about the world and how it works and to explore these collaboratively in great depth. Great value is placed upon the different experiences, ideas and opinions which children bring to discussions. Children's ideas are respected and taken seriously by the adults and by fellow children, thereby creating an environment in which children are unafraid of making mistakes or of reconstructing their own ideas. Self-confidence and self-image are fostered through discussion and debate, and creativity 'emerges from multiple experiences, coupled with the well-supported development of personal resources, including a sense of freedom to venture beyond the known' (Malaguzzi 1998: 76).

In Reggio, long-term experience has shown that children can be trusted to ask the right questions (Rinaldi 2003: 2). The role of the adult is to intervene as little as possible, but to observe, to listen, to interpret and to facilitate the children's research by providing interesting and stimulating experiences and resources. These aspects are looked at in more detail in Chapter 6.

The hundred languages of expression

Under the pedagogical guidance of Loris Malaguzzi, two theories linking language and thought developed – the hundred languages of expression and the notion of the atelier. These two aspects are closely interrelated and have come to epitomise for many the essence of the Reggio Approach.

In describing the hundred languages of expression, Malaguzzi recognised all the many different ways in which children interpret the world and represent their ideas and theories. In his poem 'No Way. The Hundred is There' Malaguzzi exhorts adults to recognise and value all forms of expression and communication, including those which are difficult to record and assess.

In the Reggio Approach, listening is seen as an active verb, not a passive one. Listening gives meaning to the message and value to the person that is giving it. As Carlina Rinaldi, pedagogical consultant to Reggio Children says:

> If we believe that children are active protagonists in the knowledge building process, then the most important verb in educational practice is no longer to talk, but to listen. Listening means being open to what others have to say, listening to the hundred or more languages, with all our senses. Listening means being open to differences and recognising the value of different points of view and the interpretations of others.
>
> (Rinaldi 1999: 7)

No Way. The Hundred is There

The child
Is made of one hundred.
The child has
a hundred languages
a hundred hands
a hundred thoughts
a hundred ways of thinking
of playing, of speaking.
A hundred always a hundred
ways of listening
of marvelling, of loving
a hundred joys
for singing and understanding
a hundred worlds
to discover
a hundred worlds

to invent
a hundred worlds
to dream.
The child has
a hundred languages
(and a hundred hundred hundred more)
but they steal ninety-nine.
The school and the culture
separate the head from the body.
They tell the child:
to think without hands
to do without head
to listen and not to speak
to understand without joy
to love and to marvel
only at Easter and at Christmas.
They tell the child:
to discover the world already there
and of the hundred
they steal ninety-nine.
They tell the child:
that work and play
reality and fantasy
science and imagination
sky and earth
reason and dream
are things
that do not belong together.
And thus they tell the child
that the hundred is not there.
The child says:
No way. The hundred is there.

Loris Malaguzzi (1997a: 3)
(translated by Lella Gandini)

The atelier

The atelier is often described as the studio, workshop or laboratory and is a characteristic feature of the design of a Reggio school. Its importance can be seen in the fact that each preschool and infant–toddler centre has a main atelier, and many also have a mini-atelier attached to each classroom.

The atelier is described as 'the place of what is possible', the place for creative thinking, research and discovery. As such it epitomises the whole research-based approach to children's learning that is fundamental to Reggio. In the atelier, children master a wide range of skills and techniques including drawing, painting, modelling with clay, using information and communications technology (ICT) and musical expression. It is the place where theories are developed and ideas are re-presented using symbolic, expressive and communicative languages.

For adults, the atelier is the environment in which they learn about the different ways in which children express themselves, and where they create and reflect on the documentation which helps to make children's learning processes visible.

The role of the atelier in promoting creativity and its relationship to the other spaces in a 'Reggio school' are discussed in Chapters 3 and 7.

Documentation

Documentation is not a final summary of a project, but an ongoing record of the process of learning and a tool for predicting and planning for what might happen next in children's learning. Central to the whole process of documentation is the detailed recording of children's activities through written notes, transcripts of conversations and discussions, audio recordings, drawings, three-dimensional (3-D) representations, photographs and video recordings. Reflecting on, and sharing, documentation with colleagues provides multiple perspectives and interpretations which support the knowledge-building process.

This aspect of the Reggio Approach is developed more fully in Chapter 8.

The importance of relationships

The Reggio philosophy is based upon reciprocal relationships which value others' opinions, viewpoints and interpretations and emphasise the importance of adults and children learning together. Collegiality, between educators, parents and children, is highly valued and well supported, and the concept of the 'learning group' is an important aspect of the Reggio Approach (Giudici *et al.* 2001: 154). The staff work in pairs, guided by a pedagogista, whose role it is to advise on appropriate learning opportunities for individual children's developmental stages, and to facilitate group learning. Each of the preschools works with an atelierista, a practising artist, there to stimulate and nurture the curiosity and creativity of the children and to act as an enabler in the development of projects.

Staff roles, organisation and continuous professional development are looked at in more detail in Chapter 2.

The role of parents in their children's education is valued and supported. Parents are expected to be active participants in the educational system, and teachers respect the views and opinions of parents. They see this as a vital part of helping to define the future direction of the whole educational experience in Reggio, particularly now that there are an increasing number of families from different cultural backgrounds (Musatti 2004). Parents also play an important role in the management of the preschools and infant–toddler centres. In January 1993, the rights of children, teachers and parents were formalised by Loris Malaguzzi in a Charter of Rights which set out the expectations and responsibilities of all parties (Malaguzzi 1997b: 214).

In Reggio, the concept of relationship extends beyond relationships between people to encompass relationships with the environment and resources as well as the relationship between the preschools and infant–toddler centres and the community of Reggio Emilia.

Such importance is placed upon the quality of the physical environment and the resources provided that reference is made to 'the environment as the third teacher'. In the schools, children work with a range of natural resources and unusual and interesting recycled materials that stimulate exploration, imagination and creativity. The role of these resources is to pose questions leading to investigation and discovery, rather than to suggest restricted activities. The interaction between the environment, children and the resources they use is regarded as an important 'relationship' within the Reggio philosophy.

The city takes great pride in the work of the preschools, and the relationship between the schools and the city of Reggio Emilia plays a vital role in children's learning about participation, citizenship and democracy. In the words of Elena Giacopini, member of the pedagogical team, 'Education should occupy public spaces and not be solely within the walls of the institution. Reggio schools are set within the City, and are visible to the City. The City of the children, the City for the children' (Giacopini 2000).

These aspects of the Reggio Approach will be looked at in more detail in Chapter 4.

The use of space

One of the most striking features of the Reggio preschools and infant–toddler centres is the physical environment and the use of space, light and colour. Not all of the preschools in Reggio are purpose-built – many exist in carefully refurbished buildings – but all are designed to maximise the potential of space and light and to be flexible and adaptable in use. The buildings provide spaces for children that are beautiful, personal and welcoming. Spaces are created which enable children to develop their potential, abilities and curiosity through exploration and research, alone and with others.

The classrooms are arranged off a central piazza – a light, open space at the heart of the school – a place for encounters, meetings, play and performance. Each school has an atelier, the creative and discovery area where children work on extended projects, developing their investigative and creative skills and theories. The dining room is at the heart of the school, and the kitchen area is visible at all times, reflecting the importance placed upon preparing and sharing food.

The symbiotic relationship which exists between architecture and the pedagogy and philosophy of the Reggio Approach is the subject of an ongoing research project between Reggio Children and the Domus Academy in Milan (Ceppi and Zini 1998).

This aspect of the Reggio Approach is developed further in Chapter 3.

The management of time

Within the Reggio philosophy, the use of time is a key factor in supporting children's learning. Through careful attention to the organisation of the day and the working week, priority is given to setting aside the necessary time for children and adults to become fully engaged in cooperative learning and building relationships. Children are given time for ideas and theories, time for discussion and debate, time for reflection, time for 'doing', time to re-visit and re-interpret, time for eating, for sleeping, time just to 'be'. Adults have time to document, time to reflect, time to interpret, time to share with colleagues and time to share with parents.

Respect is given to children's natural curiosity and creativity and their ability to produce powerful theories about the world and how it works. Many of these theories become the basis for long-term projects which provide opportunities for children to express their ideas, reflect, discuss and question, and advance their own understanding.

The trigger for a long-term project – the provocation – may come directly from an experience or encounter which the children have had, or, on occasion, from a proposition made by one of the staff. The next stage involves extended discussion so that adults and children can share ideas, information, theories, attitudes and intelligences and begin to predict what might happen next.

The organisation of the day and planning long-term projects is considered in detail in Chapter 5.

The Malaguzzi Centre and the *Hundred Languages* exhibition

In 1998, the Reggio Commune (Municipality) acquired the former Locatelli cheese factory premises as part of a scheme to regenerate the northern part of the city. In February 2006, the Loris Malaguzzi International Centre was opened in the building; it was created as a dedicated meeting place where professional development and research meet for the people of Reggio Emilia, Italy and the rest of the world.

The International Centre is a tribute to the life and work of Loris Malaguzzi who first suggested such a place should exist (International Students and Professors Study Group 2006). It was designed as a place where children and their potential would be at the forefront, and where opportunities to be creative would be offered to children, young people and families. The Centre welcomes the international educational community and all those who are engaged in innovation and education across the world, and hosts the study tours.

In 2008 *The Hundred Languages of Children* exhibition was extended to create a new exhibition showing the evolution and continuity of the documentation of children's learning in Reggio Emilia from 1981 to 2008. The exhibition was initially renamed *Ariadne's Thread*, which was Malaguzzi's preference for the title of the very first exhibition in Reggio (Pace 2008), and then took on its current title *The Wonder of Learning* in 2009.

The Malaguzzi Centre now houses several exhibitions, an auditorium and exhibition hall, a research and innovation space, the Reggio

Children bookshop, and a cafeteria and restaurant. The Centre also incorporates a preschool and primary class.

Summary

The philosophy and pedagogy of the preschools and infant–toddler centres of Reggio Emilia are distinct and clearly reflect their very particular context and origins. Across the world, early childhood educators draw insight and inspiration from deepening their understanding of the Reggio Approach, leading them to reflect on how it might influence their principles and practice. In his foreword to *The Reggio Emilia Approach – Advanced Reflections*, Howard Gardner of Harvard University writes:

> It is tempting to romanticise Reggio Emilia. It looks so beautiful, it works so well. That would be a mistake. It is clear that Reggio has struggled much in the past and that, indeed, conflict can never be absent from the achievements of any dynamic entity . . . . Political struggles at the municipal, provincial and national levels never cease, and even the wonderful start achieved by the youngsters is threatened by a secondary and tertiary educational system that is far less innovative. Reggio is distinguished less by the fact that it has found a permanent solution to these problems, because of course it has not, than by the fact that it recognises such dilemmas unblinkingly and continues to attempt to deal with them seriously and imaginatively. Reggio epitomises for me an education that is effective and humane; its students undergo a sustained apprenticeship in humanity, one that may last a lifetime.
>
> (Gardner 1998: xvii)

As Carlina Rinaldi says '(Reggio) is not a miracle; it is a huge investment in commitment' (Rinaldi 2004).

Key points

1. The historical, social, political and cultural context is a major factor in the development of the Reggio Approach.
2. The early preschools were built by local families and communities in a period of adversity and hardship.
3. The network of preschools and infant–toddler centres has evolved and developed over a period of 40 years.

4. There is no predetermined curriculum – educators describe their approach as a long-term educational project.
5. In Reggio there is a powerful image of the child as strong, competent and confident.
6. The Reggio Approach places great emphasis on the many different languages of expression that children use.
7. The atelier is viewed as 'the place of what is possible', reinforcing the importance of creative, research-based learning for children and adults.
8. Group, as well as individual, learning is valued and relationships in the widest sense are emphasised and supported.
9. Documentation is used to ensure planning is both reflective and responsive.
10. The organisation of time and space are key features which support the learning process.

Reflections on the Reggio Approach

1. Vision and values:
   - Do you have a clear, succinct vision of what you are trying to achieve?
   - Do you have an agreed set of shared values which support this vision?
   - How often do you revisit these?
2. Origins and influences:
   - How aware are you and your colleagues of the influences that shape your philosophy and practice?
   - Can you 'tell the story' of the institution you work in?
   - How important is it to keep this story alive through regularly revisiting and retelling?
3. Image of the child:
   - What is your image of the child?
   - Do you and your colleagues have an agreed, collective image?
   - How do you communicate this image to children?
   - How do you communicate this image to parents?
4. Relationships with parents:
   - Why do you want parents to be involved in the work of your setting?
   - How do you communicate this to them?
   - How do you show that you value partnership with parents?

5. Relationships with colleagues:
   - How good are you at valuing someone else's point of view?
   - What strategies do you find useful when giving, and receiving, constructive criticism?
   - Do you make full use of the support networks to which you belong?

Note

1. *Reggio Tutta: A Guide to the City by the Children* © Municipality of Reggio Emilia – Infant–Toddler Centres and Preschools, published by Reggio Children, Reggio Emilia, 2000, p. 50.

References

Achtner, W. (1994) 'Obituary: Loris Malaguzzi'. *The Independent*. Available online at www.independent.co.uk/news/people/obituary-loris-malaguzzi-1367204.html (last accessed September 2014).

Barazzoni, R. (2000) *Brick by Brick: The History of the 'XXV Aprile' People's Nursery School of Villa Cella* (English edition), Reggio Children, Reggio Emilia.

Barsotti, C. (2004) 'Walking on threads of silk', Interview with Loris Malaguzzi, *Children in Europe*, 6, 10–15.

Bonazzi, R. (2006) Personal notes from International Students and Professors Study Group. Opening of the Loris Malaguzzi International Centre.

Borghi, J. (2004) Address at the Crossing Boundaries International Conference, February, Reggio Emilia.

Ceppi, G. and Zini, M. (eds) (1998) *Children, Spaces and Relations: Metaproject for an Environment for Young Children*, Reggio Children, Reggio Emilia.

Filippini, T. and Vecchi, V. (eds) (1997) 'Historical and cultural notes on the Reggio Emilia experience', in *The Hundred Languages of Children: Narrative of the Possible*, Reggio Children, Reggio Emilia, pp. 19–21.

FixQuotes (sourced 2014) 'Facts about Loris Malaguzzi'. Available online at http://fixquotes.com/authors/loris-malaguzzi.htm (last accessed September 2014).

Gardner, H. (1998) 'Complementary perspectives on Reggio Emilia', Foreword in Edwards, C., Gandini, L. and Forman, G. (eds) *The Hundred Languages of Children: The Reggio Emilia Approach – Advanced Reflections* (2nd edn), Albex, Stamford, CT, pp. xv–xviii.

Giacopini, E. (2000) 'Historical, cultural and pedagogical aspects of the Reggio Emilia Municipal Infant–Toddler and Preschool Experience'. Seminar presentation to UK Study Group, October.

Giudici, C., Rinaldi, C. and Krechevsky, M. (eds) (2001) 'Looking closely at the group', Notes on pedagogical research, in *Making Learning Visible: Children as Individual and Group Learners*, Reggio Children, Reggio Emilia, pp. 154–6.

Hoyuelos, A. (2004) 'A pedagogy of transgression', *Children in Europe*, 6, 8.

International Students and Professors Study Group (2006) Opening of the Loris Malaguzzi International Centre.

Malaguzzi, L. (1997a) 'No way. The hundred is there', in Filippini, T. and Vecchi, V. (eds) *The Hundred Languages of Children: Narrative of the Possible*, Reggio Children, Reggio Emilia, p. 3.

Malaguzzi, L. (1997b) 'A charter of rights', in Filippini, T. and Vecchi, V. (eds) *The Hundred Languages of Children: Narrative of the Possible*, Reggio Children, Reggio Emilia, pp. 214–15.

Malaguzzi, L. (1998) 'History, ideas and basic philosophy', in Edwards, C., Gandini, L. and Forman, G. (eds) *The Hundred Languages of Children: the Reggio Emilia Approach – Advanced Reflections* (2nd edn), Albex, Stamford, CT, pp. 49–97.

Malaguzzi, L. (2000) 'When we got the news', in Barazzoni, R. *Brick by Brick: The History of the 'XXV Aprile' People's Nursery School of Villa Cella* (English edition), Reggio Children, Reggio Emilia, pp. 13–15.

Mantovani, S. (2004) Personal notes from address at the Crossing Boundaries International Conference, February, Reggio Emilia.

Musatti, T. (2004) Address at the Crossing Boundaries International Conference, February, Reggio Emilia.

Pace, M. (2008) UK Study Tour, personal communication.

Piccinini, S. (2004) 'A transforming city', *Children in Europe*, 6, 4–5.

Piccinini, S. (2006) 'Reggio Emilia – the city today, a city that is changing', International Students and Professors Study Group.

Reggio Children (1999) *The Municipal Infant–Toddler Centres and Preschools of Reggio Emilia: Historical Notes and General Information*, Reggio Children, Reggio Emilia.

Rinaldi, C. (1999) 'Visible listening', *rechild*, 3, 7, Reggio Children.

Rinaldi, C. (2003) 'The teacher as researcher', *Innovations*, 10 (2), 1–4.

Rinaldi, C. (2004) Personal notes from Crossing Boundaries International Conference, February, Reggio Emilia.

Rinaldi, C. (2006) 'Malaguzzi and the teachers', in *In Dialogue with Reggio Emilia – Listening, Researching and Learning*, Routledge, Abingdon, pp. 59, 60.

Smith, C. (1998) 'Children with special rights in pre-primary schools and infant toddler centres of Reggio Emilia', in Edwards, C., Gandini, L. and Forman, G. (eds) *The Hundred Languages of Children: the Reggio Emilia Approach – Advanced Reflections* (2nd edn), Albex, Stamford, CT, pp. 199–214.

2 The organisation of the preschools and infant–toddler centres

Reggio Emilia is big because lots of houses fit in it, and that way we can be friends with other people.[1]

We think of a school for young children as an integral living organism, as a place of shared lives and relationships among many adults and very many children.

(Malaguzzi 1998: 62)

This chapter gives an overview of the range of early childhood services in the city of Reggio Emilia, including the municipal preschools and infant–toddler centres. The roles of the 'Preschools and Infant–Toddler Centres Institution' and the Reggio Children organisation are outlined. Details of the day-to-day organisation of a typical preschool and infant–toddler centre are described, including staffing structures, work patterns and arrangements for children with additional needs. Finally, the different roles of the teacher, the atelierista and the pedagogista in supporting children's learning are discussed.

Early childhood services in Reggio Emilia

The network of municipal preschools and infant–toddler centres which exists in Reggio Emilia today has developed from the community-led preschools established immediately after the Second World War and the municipal early childhood services opened in the 1960s. Throughout their history, these municipal schools have existed alongside state and private preschools, and for more than a decade the three sectors have worked collaboratively to strengthen the range and quality of services available to families.

The population of the city of Reggio Emilia has grown considerably in the last 10 years and early childhood provision has developed in parallel. Families seeking preschool education can choose from a range of municipal, state and private providers; currently there is a total of 56 preschools, of which 23 are municipal, 12 are state and 21 are private and run by the Italian Federation of Private Preschools (FISM). All families requesting a preschool place for children aged 3 to 6 years can be accommodated. Several municipal and state school buildings have been newly built, renovated or extended in recent years to increase the number of available places. Since 2002 the enrolment arrangements for municipal and state preschools have been aligned, and a comprehensive guide to the early childhood services in Reggio Emilia is sent to all parents with children of the appropriate age to enable them to make an informed choice of preschool provision for their child (Reggio Commune 2002).

Services for children aged 3 months to 3 years are predominantly within the municipal infant–toddler centres, of which there are currently 25. Private provision is available in three centres. Developments in recent years have meant that there are now sufficient infant–toddler places for children under 3 years of age to meet parental demand (Piccinini 2006).

To support the collaborative arrangements between sectors, professional development initiatives are arranged for all teachers of 3- to 6-year-olds and all are able to access the municipal services provided by the Documentation and Research Centre, the Gianni Rodari Theatre Workshop and REMIDA Creative Recycling Centre.

Istituzione Scuola e Nidi d'Infanzia

In October 2003, the Municipality of Reggio Emilia created a new management structure for the network of municipal infant–toddler centres and preschools through the establishment of the Preschools and Infant–Toddler Centres Institution (Istituzione Scuola e Nidi d'Infanzia). The Istituzione Scuola e Nidi d'Infanzia receives 16 per cent of the Municipality's budget to provide services for children from birth to 6 years of age (Piccinini 2006).

The board of directors of the Istituzione is responsible for the ongoing development of early childhood establishments, ensuring that they are 'places which give value to children's educational rights and promote a culture of childhood based on the recognition of the ability and potential of all children'.

The network includes preschools and infant–toddler centres which are run directly by the Municipality or by affiliated cooperatives. Belonging to the Istituzione Scuola e Nidi d'Infanzia are:

- 23 preschools (of which 2 are affiliated)
- 25 infant–toddler centres (of which 11 are affiliated cooperatives)
- 600 staff (teaching and other)
- 45 school buildings.

The two affiliated preschools, known as Green Centres, have their own special identity based on the environmental aspects of the countryside in which they are located. They are also distinct in that children can attend from 2 years of age (Reggio Commune 2003).

The Loris Malaguzzi Centre incorporates a preschool and a primary class.

Community–Early Childhood Council of the infant–toddler centres and preschools

Parents have always been actively involved in the development and management of the early childhood settings of Reggio Emilia. They are represented on the Community–Early Childhood Council of each setting along with community members, teachers, staff and the pedagogical coordinator. The Council is elected every 3 years and is responsible for promoting family participation in the work of the infant–toddler centres and preschools. The whole Council meets five or six times a year and has separate committees which deal with special projects as they arise. The Council does not have direct decision-making powers, but it has an important advisory role which influences the decisions and choices made within the system. The Council also organises special events and initiatives that encourage and strengthen family participation (Reggio Children 1999: 19; Gambetti *et al.* 2003).

Reggio Children

The Reggio Children organisation, formed in March 1994, grew from an idea proposed by Loris Malaguzzi in response to the rapidly growing international interest in the work of the early childhood institutions of Reggio Emilia. Reggio Children was established as the International Centre for the Defence and Promotion of the Rights and Potential of All Children. Constituted as a limited company with mixed public and private funding, the majority shareholder is the Municipality of Reggio Emilia in association with various regional bodies, cooperatives and private businesses.

As well as supporting the work of the preschools and infant–toddler centres, Reggio Children is involved in national and international research projects on childhood and education, consultation and cooperation with projects in developing countries, professional development – including national and international seminars and study tours, support for the development of new childhood services, publishing and exhibitions. Reggio Children played a pivotal role in the development of the Loris Malaguzzi International Centre and continues to do so. Reggio Children manages the publication of the many beautiful books which illustrate the work of the infant–toddler centres and preschools, and distributes the e-magazine and newsletters *rechild* through its website www.reggio children.it. In addition, it also manages the REMIDA recycling project which has its own international outreach network (Reggio Children 2004).

Organisation of the infant–toddler centres and preschools

Staff organisation

Commitment to collegiality, respectful relationships, exchange of ideas and shared responsibility underpins the staffing structure of all the infant–toddler centres and preschools (Filippini 2001: 52). Work shifts are arranged so that the entire staff are present during the morning hours when the centres and schools are most active. Staffing schedules are organised to allow opportunities for staff to meet together and share observations and experiences on a daily and a weekly basis.

The school year

The infant–toddler centres and preschools are open for children from 1 September to 30 June with a 2-week break at Christmas and a 1-week break at Easter. Every year a number of infant–toddler centres and preschools remain open for the month of July for parents who make a special request for this facility.

All staff work for 1 week in July and 1 week in August, when children are not present, to provide time for reorganisation of the physical space, planning for reopening and meetings with parents.

The school day

The standard school day runs from 9.00 am until 3.30 pm. An extended day, from 7.30 am until 6.20 pm, is available for working parents.

Within the infant–toddler centres and preschools there are few fixed points in the day – arrival, 'morning assembly', lunch, sleep and departure. The rest of the day follows the rhythm of the children's living and learning.

Fees

Parents make a contribution towards the cost of a place in an infant–toddler centre or preschool, based on their income level. Extended day services for working parents are charged in addition to this.

In the infant–toddler centres there are five rates for fees which are charged according to the type of centre, the length of time the children spend there, and parental income.

In preschools only the additional services, such as food and transport, are charged for. Attendance at a preschool is free. There are systems in place to reduce the costs by 50 per cent for those parents who cannot afford to pay the full charge for additional services (Piccinini 2006).

Approximately 67 per cent of the total annual budget of the infant–toddler centres and preschools comes from the Municipality of Reggio Emilia, 17 per cent from parental fees and 16 per cent from other sources (Reggio Commune 2003).

The organisation of a typical infant–toddler centre

The school body

Children: 70 children	Infants (3–10 months)	12
divided into four groups:	Toddlers 1 (10–18 months)	15
	Toddlers 2 (18–24 months)	19
	Toddlers 3 (over 24 months)	24
Staff: 19 staff consisting of:	Teachers	11
	Part-time teachers (extended day)	2
	Cook	1
	Full-time assistants*	3
	Part-time assistants	3

*Cleaning staff who actively participate in the life of the school

Work schedule (36-hour week)

Teachers:	Hours with the children	31
	Professional development, community-based management, meetings with families and preparation of teaching materials	5
Cook and full-time assistants:	Normal work hours	33
	Professional development, community-based management and additional activities	3

Extended day teachers: One teacher works an 18-hour week
One teacher works a 15-hour week

Part-time helpers: 15 hours per week

Staff work shifts

Teachers Four teachers work 8.00 am to 2.00 pm
(alternating weeks): Four teachers work 8.33 am to 4.00 pm
Three teachers work 9.03 am to 4.00 pm
Extended day teacher: 3.30 pm to 6.30 pm plus one morning per week
Cook: 8.00 am to 3.20 pm
Full-time assistants One helper 8.00 am to 3.20 pm
(weekly rotation): One helper 8.30 am to 3.50 pm
One helper 9.40 am to 5.00 pm
Part-time assistants: 4.00 pm to 7.00 pm

(Work schedules will alter if families request an early arrival at 7.30 am.)
(*Source:* Reggio Children 1999: 2; UK Study Tour 2000a)

The organisation of a 3-class preschool

The school body

Children: 78 children, aged 3 to 6 years, are organised into 3 classes by age.

Staff (14) consisting of:	
Teachers	6
Part-time teacher for the extended day	1
Atelierista	1
Cook	1
Full-time assistants	2
Part-time assistants	3

Teacher work schedule (36-hour week)

Hours with the children	30
Staff meetings	2.5
Planning and professional development	1
Meeting with families	1
Documentation and preparation of materials	1.5

Staff work shifts	
Classroom teacher	
(alternating weeks):	8.00 am to 1.48 pm or 8.27 am to 4.00 pm
Extended day teacher:	3.30 pm to 7.00 pm
Atelierista:	8.30 am to 3.33 pm
Cook:	8.00 am to 3.21 pm
Full-time assistant:	8.00 am to 3.21 pm (or 9.00 am to 4.21 pm)
Part-time assistants:	One part-time assistant: 12.36 pm to 4.30 pm
	Two part-time assistants: 4.00 pm to 7.00 pm
(*Source:* Reggio Children 1999: 21; Giudici *et al.* 2001: Appendix B)	

Children with special rights

The infant–toddler centres and preschools seek to cater for children of all socio-economic backgrounds and all educational needs. In Reggio, all children are valued for their innate potential and ability, and children with disabilities are considered to have 'special rights', as opposed to 'special needs' (Smith 1998: 199). They are placed at the top of the waiting list for admission to school, and a specialist member of the pedagogical team is responsible for overseeing their overall progress.

No more than one child with special rights is allocated to any one class and, if appropriate, an extra teacher is then provided for the class. This is regarded as preferable to allocating a supporting adult to the child on a one-to-one basis. Children have a long induction period into school during which time a strategy is planned to support their ongoing development and to build up supportive relationships with the family. Observation and documentation, fundamental characteristics of the Reggio Approach, are particularly pertinent to children with special rights, as is the emphasis on collaboration and group working.

The role of the teacher

The term 'teacher' is used to refer to the majority of staff working in both the preschools and the infant–toddler centres. In the late 1960s, when the first municipal centres were proposed for children aged from 3 months to 3 years, it was necessary to overcome opposition to the concept of state provision for very young children away from their families. The infant–toddler centres were established with the remit of providing education rather than childcare for very young children, and the staff were named accordingly.

The image of the teacher in Reggio is one of a learner, enthusiastically seeking new knowledge, rather than imparting predetermined knowledge and information. Until 1998, there was no requirement in Italy for early childhood teachers to have a degree-level qualification. In-service training and staff development programmes have always been a fundamental feature of the network of Reggio schools.

This commitment to ongoing training and educational research was formally recognised in 2004 by the establishment in Reggio Emilia of the new centre for degree studies in primary education science by the Universities of Bologna and Modena (Pellacani 2004). Training is offered on two levels. The initial degree is completed in 3 years, after which students can continue to study for a further 2 years in order to gain a master's degree. The university also offers a 1-year course to support teachers working with children with special rights, which can be combined with the initial teacher training degree. Teacher training courses include subject-specific competencies, pedagogy, child psychology and educational theory, and the professional competencies needed to teach young children. Workshops and work placements are a vital part of the courses offered to emphasise the clear links between theory and practice (Cardarello 2006).

Each class of children has two teachers who work together as a team. As the children progress through the infant–toddler centre or the preschool, they stay with the same team of teachers giving the opportunity for relationships between the staff, the children and their families to be nurtured over a long period. The two teachers plan together, in collaboration with the pedagogista and atelierista, and then facilitate group working in the classrooms. They provide interesting resources and scenarios and take an active role in children's play by instigating conversations and discussions, respecting what children already know. They document children's questions and theories and act as the memory bank for the children, helping them to remember and reflect on their previous activity in order to develop their ideas further (UK Study Tour 2000b).

Throughout the day the teachers support one another in observing, documenting and interpreting the children's responses to the events and interactions which take place. These multiple perspectives on children's learning are used on a daily basis to decide what opportunities and possibilities to offer the children the following day.

Time and space for staff to meet together, to meet with parents, to plan, to document, to prepare resources and to study are recognised as vital in supporting the teachers in their role (Rinaldi 1994: 48).

The role of the pedagogista

The role of pedagogista was established in the 1970s at the time when the Municipality of Reggio first took on responsibility for developing early childhood education services. The pedagogical coordinating team oversees the work of the infant–toddler centres and preschools. The team is composed of the Director of Education, the Director of the Infant–Toddler Centres and a group of pedagogistas (Filippini 1998: 127).

The pedagogical team operates at both a local and a strategic level and plays a pivotal role in maintaining the coherence and the quality of the overall network. Each pedagogista has direct responsibility for a small group of infant–toddler centres and preschools, as well taking a lead on a specific aspect of the system – for example the Documentation and Research Centre, or REMIDA, the recycling centre. They spend part of their week being directly involved with the teachers, children and parents of the schools for which they are responsible, and part of their week in meetings and discussion with representatives of the Municipality, and with national and international colleagues. In this way they provide a vital link between practice and theory, sustaining and developing the philosophy, and helping to build a shared vision and understanding. Pedagogistas organise and deliver staff training, but also work with teachers on an individual level to support and extend their understanding of children's learning (UK Study Tour 2000c).

The practicalities of organisation at the level of the individual institution – work schedules, shift patterns, staff roles and responsibilities, and the organisation of the physical environment – are all the responsibility of the pedagogista. This arrangement values the importance of organisational systems, and recognises the fundamental role these systems play in underpinning the educational philosophy.

The role of the atelierista

The atelierista is a practising artist with a range of skills and expertise, who works as a permanent member of the staff of a preschool (Vecchi 1998: 139). The decision, made in the 1960s, to include the role of atelierista in the preschool structure made a very clear statement about the importance of creativity and imagination in the knowledge-building process (Vecchi 2004: 138).

Atelieristas – who may have expertise in the visual arts, music, dance, photography, technology, or have any one of a range of creative and expressive skills – support the development of long-term projects. They are there to bring an extra dimension to the school structure and to challenge conventional thinking – to create ripples. Atelieristas with particular expertise will equip their ateliers in different ways and offer diverse starting points from which to develop children's learning. In 2006, training was introduced specifically for groups of young atelieristas. The different skills and expertise of the atelieristas are shared collaboratively across the network of infant–toddler centres and preschools (International Students and Professors Study Group 2006).

Working with the teachers in the school, atelieristas plan and carry out long-term projects, make their skills and experience available to the children, and assist with the documentation process. They share responsibility with the teachers for managing the continuity of a project over time, as well as linking projects within the preschools to the wider community. In addition, atelieristas support the professional development of teachers in their own institution and other institutions in the network (UK Study Tour 2000d; Vecchi 2000). Wider dissemination of their skills and understanding of children's learning processes comes through the mentoring of projects in other parts of Italy.

The Hundred Languages of Children and *Ariadne's Thread* exhibitions provide detailed and comprehensive examples of the impact of the role of the atelierista on children's learning and their creative and cognitive development. Three exhibitions in the Loris Malaguzzi Centre, 1) *One City, Many Children*, 2) *Memories of a Present History* and 3) *Dialogue with Places* also celebrate the role of the atelierista in promoting young children's creativity. In 2007, the 'Ray of Light' atelier opened to the public in the Loris Malaguzzi Centre. Created by the atelieristas of Reggio Emilia, the atelier is a place of discovery and research, and immersion in the different effects and forms of light. It offers individuals and families a learning environment where they can discover the joys of science. The Centre also includes new 'Urban Ateliers' and space dedicated to food. The latter is known as the 'Atelier of Tastes'.

Subsequent chapters will look in more detail at the way in which the organisation and management of the early childhood institutions, and the various roles played by different members of staff, contribute to the philosophy and pedagogy of the Reggio Approach.

Key points

1. The municipal, state and private schools work collaboratively to provide early childhood services for children aged 3 months to 6 years old.
2. Parents have always been actively involved in the development and management of early childhood services in Reggio.
3. A commitment to collegiality, relationships, exchange of ideas, and shared responsibility underpins the staffing structure.
4. The standard school day is from 9.00 am to 3.30 pm. An extended day from 7.30 am to 6.20 pm is available for working parents.
5. Parents make a contribution towards the cost of their child's education, depending on their income level.
6. The infant–toddler centres and preschools cater for all children – those with disabilities are considered to have 'special rights' rather than 'special needs'.
7. Teachers are viewed as enthusiastic learners and researchers rather than imparters of received knowledge.
8. Each group of children has two teachers who remain with them throughout their time in the infant–toddler centre or preschool.
9. The pedagogista operates at both local and strategic levels, supporting teachers, parents and the network of centres in developing children's learning.
10. The role of the atelierista – a practising artist who supports the development of children's learning, creativity and imagination – is central to the Reggio Approach.

Reflections on the Reggio Approach

1. Staff collegiality:
   - Consider the nature of teams within your setting. What different teams exist and how do they operate?
   - Is everyone aware of their individual and collective roles and responsibilities?
   - Do different teams communicate effectively?

2. Parental involvement:
   - How are parents involved in your setting?
   - Is parental consultation valued and acted upon?
   - Do parents have an opportunity to share their skills and expertise?
3. The role of the practitioner:
   - How is the role of the practitioner viewed in your setting?
   - What opportunities do staff have to share their expertise and experience?
   - Who is responsible for ensuring the continuing professional development of all staff?
4. The role of the atelierista:
   - As a staff team, how do you identify and nurture your own creativity?
   - Could individuals use their talents and interests to develop a similar role to that of the atelierista?
5. Children with special rights:
   - Consider the notion of children with 'special rights' rather than 'special needs'. How do you view children with additional needs?
   - How do you ensure all children have the opportunity to express their creativity and to explore the world around them?

Note

1. *Reggio Tutta: A Guide to the City by the Children* © Municipality of Reggio Emilia – Infant–Toddler Centres and Preschools, published by Reggio Children, Reggio Emilia, 2000, p. 33.

References

Cardarello, R. (2006) 'The role of the university in the town of Reggio Emilia', International Students and Professors Study Group.

Filippini, T. (1998) 'The role of the pedagogista', in Edwards, C., Gandini, L. and Forman, G. (eds) *The Hundred Languages of Children: The Reggio Emilia Approach – Advanced Reflections* (2nd edn), Albex, Stamford, CT, pp. 127–37.

Filippini, T. (2001) 'On the nature of organisation', in Giudici, C., Rinaldi, C. and Krechevsky, M. (eds) *Making Learning Visible: Children as Individual and Group Learners*, Reggio Children, pp. 52–7.

Gambetti, A., Ricco, P. and Vercalli, E. (eds) (2003) *The Charter of the City and Childhood Councils. The Notebooks No.7*, Reggio Children, Reggio Emilia.

Giudici, C., Rinaldi, C. and Krechevsky, M. (eds) (2001) *Making Learning Visible: Children as Individual and Group Learners*, Reggio Children, Reggio Emilia.

International Students and Professors Study Group (2006) Notes.

Malaguzzi, L. (1998) 'History, ideas and basic philosophy', in Edwards, C., Gandini, L. and Forman, G. (eds) *The Hundred Languages of Children: The Reggio Emilia Approach – Advanced Reflections* (2nd edn), Albex, Stamford, CT, pp. 49–97.

Pellacani, C. (2004) Address at Crossing Boundaries International Conference, February, Reggio Emilia.

Piccinini, S. (2006) 'Reggio Emilia – the city today, a city that is changing', International Students and Professors Study Group.

Reggio Children (1999) *The Municipal Infant–Toddler Centres and Preschools of Reggio Emilia. Historical Notes and General Information*, Reggio Emilia.

Reggio Children (2004) Information booklet 'Reggio Children', Crossing Boundaries International Conference, February, Reggio Emilia.

Reggio Commune (2002) 'School for children aged 3–6 in Reggio Emilia'. Supplement in *Reggio Commune no.1*, January.

Reggio Commune (2003) 'Preschool for children enrolments 2004–2005 school year'. Supplement in *Reggio Commune no.12*, December.

Rinaldi, C. (1994) 'Staff development in Reggio Emilia', in Katz, L.G. and Cesarone, B. (eds) *Reflections on the Reggio Emilia Approach. Perspectives from ERIC/EECE*, University of Illinois, Cat. No. 215.

Smith, C. (1998) 'Children with "special rights" in the pre-primary schools and infant–toddler centres of Reggio Emilia', in Edwards, C., Gandini, L. and Forman, G. (eds) *The Hundred Languages of Children: The Reggio Emilia Approach – Advanced Reflections* (2nd edn), Albex, Stamford, CT, pp. 199–214.

UK Study Tour (2000a) Identity cards of the Alice and Bellelli municipal infant–toddler centres.

UK Study Tour (2000b) 'Relationship between the school and the environment in respect of a day in the life of a school'. Presentation to UK Study Group, October.

UK Study Tour (2000c) Notes from visit to Diana municipal preschool.

UK Study Tour (2000d) Notes from visit to Allende municipal preschool.

Vecchi, V. (1998) 'The role of the atelierista', in Edwards, C., Gandini, L. and Forman, G. (eds) *The Hundred Languages of Children: The Reggio Emilia Approach – Advanced Reflections* (2nd edn), Albex, Stamford, CT, pp. 139–47.

Vecchi, V. (2000) 'The curtain of the Ariosto Theatre'. Seminar presentation to UK Study Group, October.

Vecchi, V. (2004) 'Poetic languages as a means to counter violence', in Vecchi, V. and Giudici, C. (eds) *Children, Art, Artists. The Expressive Languages of Children: The Artistic Language of Alberto Burri*, Reggio Children, Reggio Emilia, pp. 137–43.

3 The environment

In San Prospero Square you can see the lions. In fact, it's also called the Lion Square. They're stone lions. They're really special! They're made of orange-colored stone and they're real big because they even have a place where the kids can sit on them. In fact, they put the lions there for the kids to have fun on.[1]

We should not be afraid of making schools that are too beautiful; care and attention to the environment should not be regarded as educational waste or a non-essential aesthetic adjunct.

(Vecchi 2002: 12)

This chapter looks at the principles that lie behind the design of spaces for early childhood in Reggio. The layout and spatial organisation of a typical infant–toddler centre or preschool is described to show how these design features are put into practice, indoors and out of doors. The use of space is then exemplified by descriptions of two visits, one to a purpose-built infant–toddler centre, and the other to a preschool in a converted villa.

The spaces which children, educators and parents inhabit are a significant feature of the Reggio Approach; the quality of the environment is both an expectation and an entitlement. The architecture and layout of the preschools and infant–toddler centres reflect the aesthetics of their surroundings, emphasising space, light, form and colour. The piazzas, ateliers and courtyards reflect the squares, galleries, museums and parks of the city itself.

In Reggio there is a belief that children have a right to a rich, complex environment that provides a wealth of sensory experiences. In the words of Loris Malaguzzi: 'Our objective, which we will always pursue, is to create an available environment in which children, families and teachers feel at ease' (Malaguzzi 1998: 61).

The concepts of time and space are closely interrelated, with the physical environment regarded as a partner in the learning process. The design of the preschool and infant–toddler centre buildings reflects the encounter between pedagogy and architecture and has been a topic for research between the Domus Academy of Milan and Reggio Children for many years (Ceppi and Zini 1998).

The aim of this research project, involving educators, artists, architects and engineers is to: 'enable a meeting of minds between the avant-garde pedagogical philosophy of Reggio Emilia preschools and innovative experiences within the culture and design of architecture' (Zini 1998).

Every space has a purpose

The preschool and infant–toddler centre buildings in Reggio incorporate large open spaces, small spaces, thresholds and outdoor environments, all of which serve well-thought-out, clearly identified, purposes.

For **children** spaces are created where they can:

- express themselves
- explore and investigate

- think and reflect
- be involved in projects
- reinforce their identities
- communicate
- feel their identity and privacy is respected.

For **educators** there are spaces in which they can:

- meet with other adults to share experiences and observations
- study and research
- have privacy.

For **parents** spaces are designed to enable them to:

- engage with their children's learning
- hear and be heard
- meet with others
- participate in the life of the school.

Design features

The synergy between the design features and the pedagogy highlights the architectural aspects of circularity, relationships and communication within the infant–toddler centres and preschool buildings (Rinaldi 1998: 114).

Light, shadow and reflection

One of the most striking features is the use of light sources, both natural and artificial. Windows are large and placed to facilitate the child's view both of the outside world and of the internal spaces in the building. The windows give vistas and interesting glimpses of the outside world from within. Artificial light levels can be varied to facilitate investigation of the interplay of light and shadow through the use of shadow screens and light tables. Reflective surfaces – mirrors on the walls, at right angles to one another and arranged in triangular prisms – provide unusual viewpoints and prompt reflection, both literal and metaphorical.

Connectivity

Visibility and interconnectedness are concepts that underpin the internal designs, linking internal spaces together and connecting the inside with the outside. The piazza is the central space of the school shared by children, parents and teachers. The piazza reflects the image of the city of Reggio Emilia, a place for encounters and journeys which changes with the rhythm of the day, the week and the year. The atelier, classrooms, dining room and kitchen are physically attached to the piazza and are visible from it.

Materials and finishes

Colours are subtle and are chosen to give a varied landscape, with not too much stimulation. Vibrant colours are reserved for large structural pieces of equipment such as kaleidoscope mirrors, dressing-up capsules and shadow theatres. Materials and finishes are carefully selected for their aesthetic, sensorial and functional qualities in order to create an environment which is culturally appropriate for babies and young children. Particular attention is paid to floors, ceilings and walls, those aspects of the building with which young children are the most familiar (Rinaldi 1998: 119).

Flexibility and adaptability

The buildings, inside and out, are designed to be inhabited and changed over time, by children with different identities and different cultural and social mores. Each year, groups of children move to different rooms within the infant–toddler centre or preschool building. These rooms will have particular characteristics and features – traces of their previous occupants – but are designed to be adaptable to meet the needs and confirm the identities of the incoming group of children (UK Study Tour 2000a).

Multi-sensorial

Integral to the design and construction of the different spaces is an appreciation of the importance of children and adults experiencing the world through all their senses. Children are able to vary the light levels in different areas and are encouraged to be aware of the tactile, acoustic and olfactory properties of the different environments they inhabit.

Spaces within a preschool or infant–toddler centre

The same basic design features are found in all of the preschools and infant–toddler centres, whether they are purpose-built or redesigned spaces built originally for another purpose. A typical purpose-built centre would include the following arrangement of spaces:

Piazza

This is a large, open space at the heart of the building where much of the large-scale equipment, including the dressing-up capsule and kaleidoscope mirror, is located. It is a place for meetings and encounters between children of different ages and is the space one passes through on the way to the other rooms in the building.

Atelier

The atelier, located off the piazza, is a place of experimentation and discovery. It epitomises Malaguzzi's concept of the whole school as an environment for participation, research and creative expression where children and adults learn from, and alongside, one another (Malaguzzi 1998: 75). In Reggio, creativity is not considered as a distinct aptitude, but rather as a characteristic way of thinking, making choices and solving problems. 'Creativity becomes more visible when adults try to be more attentive to the cognitive processes of children than to the results they achieve in various fields of doing and understanding' (Malaguzzi 1998: 77).

The atelier may contain specialised equipment and resources, but it is not considered a self-contained area dissociated from the rest of the school. Instead it is a physical manifestation of the value of visual expression and language. In explaining the concept of the atelier, Vea Vecchi, atelierista, describes the importance of visual language as a means of enquiry and investigation of the world. She sees it as a way of building bridges and relationships between different experiences and languages, and of keeping cognitive and expressive processes in close relationship with one another. The emphasis is on the constant dialogue with a pedagogical approach that seeks to work on the connections between, rather than the separation of, different fields of knowledge (Vecchi 2004: 137).

In the words of Sergio Spaggiari, director of the Istituzione Scuola e Nidi d'Infanzia: 'Science may dance with art, maths sing with music, logic ride with ethics' (Spaggiari 2004).

Classrooms

The classrooms are arranged off the central piazza and have direct access to the outdoors. They are flexible spaces, equipped with low platform areas for group meetings, light tables, pull-down screens and construction areas. Each has a second space, the mini-atelier attached to it, designed to bring creative activity into the day-to-day activities of the children. Wherever possible, a third area exists within the classroom, which is often designated by the children as a 'quiet zone' with low light levels (Vecchi 1998: 132).

Dining room and kitchen

These spaces are considered to be as important as all the other spaces in the school. The work of the cooks is highly valued, and this respect reflects the history and traditions of Reggio Emilia which demonstrate that the preparation and presentation of food is an integral part of social relationships in the city.

Mealtimes are opportunities for self-sufficiency, social interaction and friendship in an environment which supports the cognitive and emotional development of the children. The kitchen is located next to the dining area and is visible through large windows. Children are encouraged to appreciate the time and care which goes into the preparation of food and to enjoy the multi-sensory experience of 'the good smelling kitchen' (Strozzi and Vecchi 2002: 23).

The close proximity of the kitchens and cooks to the places inhabited by the children encourages the development of ideas and projects.

So it happens that the children invent recipes for ghosts and for birthday cakes; they prepare dishes from their grandparents' recipes or make theme-based snacks for their friends, establishing the work procedures for measuring the ingredients; they design and cultivate a vegetable garden, investigate raw materials and foods to transform and rethink them with care and aesthetic sensibility.

(Cavallini and Tedeschi 2008: 22)

In the preschools the children spend time each day setting the tables for lunch. One of the children often 'oversees' the work as cloths are laid, places are set, with all actions carefully sequenced (International Students and Professors Study Group 2006). In *The Languages of Food* a project is described where a 'Table Setting Handbook' is prepared by the 5-year-olds as a legacy for the 4-year-olds (Cavallini and Tedeschi 2008: 24).

Internal courtyard

This 'room without a roof' is located off the piazza, and is clearly visible through large, full-length windows. It provides a bridge between the inside and the outside and heightens awareness of the time of day, the weather and the seasons.

Outdoor spaces

The outdoor areas typically contain large wooden play structures, areas for play and performance, and shaded picnic tables and benches. Indoor activities are frequently taken outside to add a new dimension, and children have free access to the outdoor area, with the permission of the teacher (UK Study Tour 2000a). Large-scale constructions exist in the grounds of some of the schools – a climbing tower, amphitheatre or terraced seating area, for example.

In the grounds of La Villetta preschool is an outdoor atelier where creative resources are laid out for the children under a covered wooden pergola. Half of the atelier space is set out as an artist's studio with easels, a table and beautifully presented drawing, painting and modelling tools and materials. The other half of the outdoor atelier is a place where children explore natural materials, including driftwood, stones, rocks and sand. These are laid out exquisitely in grey utilitarian trays from a builders' merchants. A set of shelves painted in the same neutral shade of grey holds the equipment which children use to enhance their investigations – sieves, funnels, scales and timers. The neutral shades of the outdoor furnishings contrast sharply with the beauty of the natural materials and the few brightly coloured pieces of equipment, giving clarity to the space and materials which the children investigate (UK Study Tour 2005).

Children's awareness of the outdoor world, the weather and the seasons is fostered by the design of the buildings and by the many long-term projects which encourage children to wonder at the beauty and complexity of their natural environment. The presence of gardens in the outdoor areas of the infant–toddler centres and preschools is an important feature of the learning environment presented to the children. In the gardens, children learn the importance of taking care of a plot of earth. They plant seeds, watch them grow and eventually harvest the fruits of their labour to be cooked and eaten. Within the gardens, meadow areas are cultivated to add to the richness of the outdoor environment. Stefano Sturloni, atelierista at the Allende preschool, talks about the gardens providing 'a fragrant future', and reminds us of the abundance of learning opportunities which the natural world provides. 'Grass: who even notices it any more? Only children, who navigate it with all the curiosity of explorers. And they are right, because if you observe closely, grass is a whole continent teeming with surprises, especially if you let it grow a bit' (Sturloni 2008).

Vivid descriptions of how the children inhabit the outdoor spaces, and indeed the school itself, are contained in the *Advisories* booklet produced by 5- and 6-year-old children in the Diana School for the new group of 3-year-olds beginning school the following September (Strozzi and Vecchi 2002).

Documentation panels

The documentation panels which line the walls are part of the fabric of the building – the 'second skin' (Crossing Boundaries 2004). They connect the present users – children, teachers and families – with the learning that is going on from day to day, and provide memories and traces of the past projects which are part of the identity of the school.

The following two sections illustrate the use of space within an infant–toddler centre and a preschool on a 'typical day'.

A visit to a purpose-built infant–toddler centre

The entrance of an infant–toddler centre is a welcoming place which invites the visitor in and encourages communication. It is the place where the centre 'introduces itself' and declares 'who we are'. The entrance displays the identity card of the school and contains a floor plan and organisational structure of the centre. It also provides information about the staff, meetings for parents and activities within the city, as well as documentation of the life of the centre.

As children arrive at the infant–toddler centre they will be waited for and welcomed by their friends through the strategically placed low windows which overlook the path to the entrance. The windows have soft furnishings next to them to encourage the toddlers inside to linger and wait for new arrivals – or perhaps to watch the birds, creating a new interest for the day.

On arrival, children and parents can look through the window and glimpse a rich variety of activity. A small group of toddlers are playing with blocks on a mat while others are testing their skills on a low set of steps, looking down onto mirrors. Small, curtained spaces encourage the children to play 'cuckoo' (peek-a-boo) – opacity is as important as transparency in these soft, light, mysterious places.

Parents do not 'drop off' their children. They enter the building together and often engage in conversation with the staff – they talk *with* the children, not *about* the children.

The next space that is entered is the piazza; this is an open space for encounters, exchanges and opportunities to meet with children of different ages. The piazza is the most 'public' space in the building and it is animated by stories that the children tell, by large communication tubes, by the dressing-up and performance areas, and by large mirrors.

In the centre of the building is an open patio area or internal courtyard, 'a room without a ceiling'. This symbolises the connection between the indoors and the outdoors. In good weather the children have free access to this space, at other times it is a 'winter garden' inside the building.

The atelier, a workshop where the children use expressive language to develop their ideas, theories and projects, offers visibility in all directions – onto the patio, the piazza and the open areas between the infant and toddler rooms.

The rooms for toddlers and infants that open off the piazza are designed to encourage encounters with the eyes, the hands and the whole body. Even the rooms for the very youngest children offer opportunities to work with clay, to construct and to experiment with playing in the light and the dark. Toddlers follow the stories in the documentation around the walls at child level; they communicate with one another by 'touching' through the glass boundaries between spaces; they observe their friends exploring in the atelier, or workshop space, through the large windows.

In the dining room, as in the rest of the building, furniture is appropriately proportioned and is chosen to reflect both the comfortable and stylish aspects of the local culture. The dining room is a dedicated space within the building because social interaction at mealtimes is seen to be an important aspect of child development.

There is little evidence of plastic – the children use glasses, ceramic plates and real knives and forks. A full-length window creates a visible link between the dining room and the kitchen, allowing children to participate in the process of food preparation. The 2- and 3-year-olds assist with the preparation of meals and snacks, set the tables and help to clear away. The visibility of the kitchen also emphasises the importance of all staff members in the centre and enables them to communicate with children and families.

In the bathrooms, multi-sensory experiences are provided through scents, mirrors, music and textures, in recognition of the theory that the body is inseparable from the mind. Children's belongings are stored in closed lockers, one metre tall, in the cloakroom area.

Sleeping areas have stacking cots, beds and padded wicker 'nests' which babies can access freely. These areas are transformed by light and dark; wall-mounted light boxes, dimmer switches and torches provide a restful atmosphere for sleep. Ceilings are softened by drapes and canopies made from lightweight, natural, coloured fabrics.

Nursing chairs are provided in the baby rooms, and staff respect parents' different schedules by encouraging breastfeeding mothers to feel welcome.

Great care and attention are given to the selection and storage of materials and resources which stimulate and enrich the very youngest children's curiosity, creativity and communication. The atelier has a system of open shelving for storage and provides a rich supply of resources for the children to access independently. These include marbles, buttons, wire, paper, scarves, beads, ceramic and glass pieces, and a wide range of natural materials. A light box and low easels are available along with clay, paint and a variety of types of sand.

Small groups of infants and toddlers can be seen playing together with natural materials – wood, pebbles, seed pods, gourds, leaves, glass bottles with coloured water, torches and the overhead projector. Together they will investigate the resources and explore the effects of light and shadow. Each child has the opportunity to develop his or her own individual learning while benefiting from the collective learning of their group (UK Study Tour 1999, 2000b).

A visit to a preschool housed in a converted villa

Several of the preschools in Reggio Emilia are housed in converted villas with the accommodation spread out over four or five floors.

While spaces have been created in keeping with the same pedagogical influence as the purpose-built preschools, there is an added dimension of the challenges and possibilities posed by the impressive staircases. These are used as pathways, delineated by stories and visual narratives which draw the visitor upwards. As the buildings are old, modifications are made to ensure the architectural context is in keeping with the educational philosophy. Floors have been raised next to windows to ensure the required degree of visibility for the children. Small, flexible spaces are created by the use of lightweight drapes and screens. Light and shadow are investigated using light boxes and the overhead projector; virtual spaces are constructed using light and shadow. Light becomes a tangible material, used for games of colour, games of mosaic, of landscape and of construction.

On the ground floor is the 3-year-olds' room, which is the home base for 26 children. Here, at this early stage in their experience of the preschool, there is a focus on the children learning about cooperation, space and togetherness, fostered through discovery arising from the children's curiosity and interests. Small groups of children are involved in experimentation, using all their senses, with the materials which have been provided for them – they discover for themselves much more than they are told. Tiered staging provides a seating area and creates an auditorium for the puppet theatre. The classroom has a play kitchen, construction area, reading area and its own bathroom. In the mini-atelier attached to the classroom, children are investigating autumn colours, and in the message area they are looking at the detail of natural objects and recording their words and thoughts.

Also on the ground floor are the entrance, the piazza, the dressing-up area, the dining area and the kitchen. The spaces for eating and food preparation are visible in the centre of the school, where the children can appreciate the quantity and quality of time which goes into the preparation and serving of food.

The piazza is the place for performance and role play, and is the home of the puppet theatre. It is a space that can be transformed by fantasy and imagination according to the interests and ideas of the children. A group of four children are using fabrics to make mosaic constructions on the floor, some temporary, some more permanent.

On the first floor, the 4-year-olds have an area dedicated to shadow play, and they are investigating how shadows change our perception of objects. In the mini-atelier the children are engaged in a long-term project on 'Birth' which was begun the previous year. They are working with clay, making models that represent their ideas about their own birth, the birth of other creatures and the origins of the cosmos.

The 5-year-olds inhabit the second floor. They have created a construction within a kaleidoscope mirror and are investigating a large periscope. The resources and equipment they are using are sophisticated and complex – inks, transparencies, large set squares and a computer. They are freely accessible and used competently and confidently by the children.

The atelier on the final floor is a complementary space to the classrooms, not an alternative. Under the guidance of the atelierista, children learn to 'qualify the hand in order to qualify the mind'. The children are using different technologies – computer, clay, wire – to further their understanding of equilibrium. One small group of children is teaching another what they have learned from their experience with robots.

Throughout the session, music is playing and one area of the school has been set out as a music atelier with a wide range of instruments for the children to investigate the qualities of sound.

Outside, a group of children have fed the birds and are now watching them from the wisteria-clad bird hide in the grounds (UK Study Tour 2000a, 2000c).

Summary

The importance that educators in Reggio place on the physical environment inhabited by children and adults is summed up in the words of Loris Malaguzzi: 'Education must come to be recognised as the product of complex interactions, many of which can be realised when the environment is a fully participating element' (Malaguzzi 1997: 40).

Two videos that comprise the DVD *Everyday Utopias*, produced and sold by Reggio Children in 2011 as part of *The Wonder of Learning* exhibition, provide visual descriptions of a day in an infant–toddler centre and a day in a preschool, which show the centres exactly as they are on a day-to-day basis. They were produced because, in the words of Malaguzzi, 'to raise normal children is the result of a hard-won and everyday utopia' (Malaguzzi 2011).

Key points

1. The architecture and the pedagogy exist in a symbiotic relationship with one another.
2. The purpose of every space is carefully considered – from the point of view of the children, the parents and the educators.
3. Light, shadow and reflection are important elements in the design and construction of environments for young children.
4. Connectivity, visibility, flexibility and adaptability are essential features in any design brief.
5. Children have a right to a rich, complex environment which provides a wealth of sensory experiences.
6. The atelier epitomises the concept of school as a place of participation, research and creative expression.
7. The kitchen and dining areas are at the heart of the school and are considered as important as all the other spaces in the school.
8. The preparation of food and the rituals surrounding mealtimes are starting points for many interesting projects.
9. Children's awareness of the beauty and complexity of the natural environment is fostered by the design and layout of the buildings.
10. Outdoor ateliers and gardens provide environments for children to explore their connectivity with the natural world.

Reflections on the Reggio Approach

1. The environment and your philosophy:
   - What is the relationship between the physical environment of your setting and your philosophy?
   - Does the environment help or hinder what you want to do?
   - What changes could you make?
2. Every space has a purpose:
   - Walk around your setting. Is it easy to 'read' the physical space?
   - Is it clear why each space is arranged as it is?
   - Do you know which spaces children, staff and parents like and dislike?
3. Design and flexibility:
   - How much attention do you pay to light, shadow, colour, texture, smell and sound?

- Do you value spaces that can be changed and adapted?
- Can the children, as well as the adults, change the spaces?

4. Food and mealtimes:
   - Are mealtimes occasions for social interaction, conversation and the appreciation of good food?
   - How often do you involve children in talking about, handling and preparing food?
   - How effectively do you encourage children to explore their environment using all their senses?

5. Indoors and outdoors:
   - Do you make full use of learning opportunities outdoors – in all weathers?
   - Are there spaces outdoors that can be changed and adapted by children in response to their current interests and preoccupations?
   - How well do you make use of gardens and growing spaces to consolidate children's understanding of the natural world?

Note

1. *Reggio Tutta: A Guide to the City by the Children* © Municipality of Reggio Emilia – Infant–Toddler Centres and Preschools, published by Reggio Children, Reggio Emilia, 2000, p. 71.

References

Cavallini, I. and Tedeschi, M. (eds) (2008) *The Languages of Food. Recipes, Experiences, Thoughts*, Reggio Children, Reggio Emilia, pp. 22, 24.

Ceppi, G. and Zini, M. (eds) (1998) *Children, Spaces, Relations. Metaproject for an Environment for Young Children*, Reggio Children, Reggio Emilia.

Crossing Boundaries (2004) Notes from a visit to Michelangelo municipal preschool.

Everyday Utopias DVD (2011) – *A Day in an Infant-Toddler Centre and a Day in a Preschool*, Reggio Children, Reggio Emilia.

International Students and Professors Study Group (2006) Notes.

Malaguzzi, L. (1997) 'The environment', in Filippini, T. and Vecchi, V. (eds) *The Hundred Languages of Children. Narrative of the Possible*, Reggio Children, Reggio Emilia.

Malaguzzi, L. (1998) 'History, ideas and basic philosophy', in Edwards, C., Gandini, L. and Forman, G. (eds) *The Hundred Languages of Children: The Reggio Emilia Approach – Advanced Reflections* (2nd edn), Albex, Stamford, CT, pp. 49–97.

Malaguzzi, L. (2011) *Everyday Utopias* DVD – *A Day in an Infant-Toddler Centre and a Day in a Preschool*, Reggio Children, Reggio Emilia.

Rinaldi, C. (1998) 'The space for childhood', in Ceppi, G. and Zini, M. (eds) *Children, Spaces, Relations. Metaproject for an Environment for Young Children*, Reggio Children, Reggio Emilia, pp. 114–20.

Spaggiari, S. (2004) Presentation at Crossing Boundaries International Conference, February, Reggio Emilia.

Strozzi, P. and Vecchi, V. (eds) (2002) *Advisories*, Reggio Children, Reggio Emilia.

Sturloni, S. (2008) 'A fragrant future', in Cavallini, I. and Tedeschi, M. (eds) *The Languages of Food. Recipes, Experiences, Thoughts*, Reggio Children, Reggio Emilia, pp. 106–7.

UK Study Tour (1999) Notes from visit to Arcobaleno infant–toddler centre.

UK Study Tour (2000a) 'Relationship between the school and the environment in respect of a day in the life of a school'. Presentation to UK Study Group, October.

UK Study Tour (2000b) Notes from visit to Alice infant–toddler centre.

UK Study Tour (2000c) Notes from visit to La Villetta municipal preschool.

UK Study Tour (2005) Notes from visit to La Villetta municipal preschool.

Vecchi, V. (1998) 'What kind of a space for living well in school?', in Ceppi, G. and Zini, M. (eds) *Children, Spaces, Relations. Metaproject for an Environment for Young Children*, Reggio Children, Reggio Emilia, pp. 128–35.

Vecchi, V. (2002) 'Grace and care as education', in *Atelier 3 Furnishings for Young Children* (English edition), ISAAF/Reggio Children, Reggio Emilia, pp. 11–12.

Vecchi, V. (2004) 'Poetic languages as a means to counter violence', in Vecchi, V. and Giudici, C. (eds) *Children, Art, Artists. The Expressive Languages of Children: The Artistic Language of Alberto Burri*, Reggio Children, Reggio Emilia, pp. 137–43.

Zini, M. (1998) 'Introduction', in Ceppi, G. and Zini, M. (eds) *Children, Spaces, Relations. Metaproject for an Environment for Young Children*, Reggio Children, Reggio Emilia.

4 Relationships

The market is shaped like a square and all the houses go around it. It's full of people. You can smell the perfume of the ladies that go by, the smells of pizza and cakes.[1]

In Reggio one is given to meeting a rare form of courtesy, a precious form of reciprocal respect.

(Bruner 2004: 27)

This chapter looks at the network of different reciprocal relationships that are such an important feature of the Reggio Approach. These include: relationships between children, supported by an emphasis on group learning; relationships with parents and the importance of parental participation; relationships between educators and the value of collegiality, cooperation and teamwork; relationships with the environment and resources; relationships between the early childhood institutions and the community of Reggio Emilia.

Reciprocal relationships

Respectful relationships lie at the heart of the approach to early childhood education within the infant–toddler centres and preschools of Reggio Emilia. The interaction between parents, children and teachers, and the relationships that are forged between them, are seen as essential elements in supporting young children's learning and development. The value placed on interaction and dialogue is a reflection of the culture of this part of Italy, with its tradition of regular and protracted discussion and debate.

Within the organisational structure of the schools, relationships are supported and reinforced by setting aside time for children to talk with teachers and with other children, for teachers to talk with teachers, atelieristas and pedagogistas, for teachers to talk with parents, and for parents to talk together. Parents are considered to be active participants in the life of the schools rather than merely being linked to them through their children. The education of young children in Reggio is truly seen as a shared responsibility in which everyone is expected to be an active participant.

Relationships are always considered to be reciprocal, requiring mutual trust and respect. This involves acknowledging everyone as a resource within his or her own culture and valuing each person's skills, differences and points of view. In a presentation during the UK Study Tour in October 2000, Carlina Rinaldi, pedagogical consultant to Reggio Children, offered a visualisation of 'the school' by defining it through the reciprocal relationships that exist between teachers, children and parents, see Figure 4.1 (Rinaldi 2000: 58).

The school sits within, and interacts with, its own cultural and social environment, and each protagonist – child, parent or teacher – brings their own values, interests, ideas and expertise, which are shared and respected by the others (Rinaldi 2000).

Relationships are valued and supported through what is termed in Reggio, 'the pedagogy of listening' (Rinaldi 1999a). Listening involves

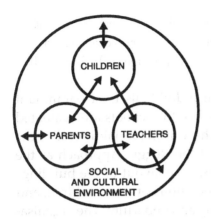

Figure 4.1 Reciprocal relationships

(Rinaldi 2000)

openness and a willingness to value the points of view of others. Listening to the theories and opinions put forward by an individual gives value to those ideas and thereby gives value to the individual. The self-esteem of both children and adults is supported and developed through knowing that their ideas, questions and explanations are important and worthy of consideration and discussion (Rinaldi 2001: 80). The concept of listening has been further developed in Reggio through the use of documentation to make listening visible and available to interpretation by a wider audience (Rinaldi 1999b: 7).

Children

The pedagogical approach in Reggio is founded on Loris Malaguzzi's image of the competent, confident child – rich in potential, strong and powerful, connected to adults and to other children (Malaguzzi 1998: 79). Children are viewed as co-constructors of knowledge, learning alongside other children and adults through working in partnership with them.

In January 1993, Malaguzzi proposed a charter of rights setting out 'The Rights of Children' alongside 'The Rights of Parents' and 'The Rights of Teachers'. 'The Rights of Children' begins with the statement:

Children have the right to be recognised as subjects of individual, civil, legal and social rights; as both source and constructors of their own experience, and thus active participants in the organisation of their identities, abilities and autonomy, through interaction with their peers, with adults, with ideas, with objects and with the real and imaginary events of intercommunicating worlds.

(Malaguzzi 1997a: 214)

The quality of the relationships between individuals is of paramount importance; all aspects of the organisation of the schools are evaluated to ensure that they support this philosophy. Carlina Rinaldi recalls how Loris Malaguzzi defined the pedagogy of the Reggio Approach as the 'pedagogy of relationships' (Rinaldi 2006). The layout of the buildings is designed to facilitate meetings and interaction between children, and great care is taken over areas for welcoming and departure. The organisation of the day allows time for encounters between children of different ages, and the emphasis on group learning reinforces the importance of considering different points of view and sharing ideas and theories.

Children's theories – the starting point for long-term projects – are developed through group discussion, and children are supported in learning to master the skills of listening and negotiation. Self-esteem and self-awareness are fostered through valuing individual opinions, respecting the knowledge children already have, welcoming doubt and uncertainty, and developing children's skills in asking good questions of themselves and others.

Children with 'special rights' play as full a part as possible in the life of the schools and all children are supported to find strategies to include their peers in day-to-day activities. Integration is supported by the collaborative approach to learning that is fostered in all the children, and by the emphasis on valuing and respecting differences (UK Study Tour 2000a).

Parents

The first preschools were founded by the parents in the period following the Second World War as a symbol of hope and the desire to build a better future for their children. Parental participation has therefore always been at the heart of the pedagogical experience within the preschools and infant–toddler centres of Reggio Emilia (Spaggiari 1998).

In discussing the origins of the preschools and the driving forces behind the evolving Reggio philosophy, Loris Malaguzzi said:

They (the parents) asked us for nothing less than that this school, which they had built with their own hands, be a different kind of school, a school that could

educate their children in a different way from before. It was the women especially who expressed this desire. The equation was simple: if the children had
legitimate rights, then they should also have the opportunities to develop their
intelligence and to be made ready for the success which would not, and should
not, escape them. These were the parents' thoughts, expressing a universal aspi-
ration, a declaration against the betrayal of children's potential, and a warning
that children, first of all, had to be taken seriously and believed in. These three
ideas could have fitted perfectly in any good book on education. They suited us
just fine. The ideas coming from parents were shared by others who understood
their deep implications. And if our endeavour has endured for many years, it
has been because of this collective wisdom.

(Malaguzzi 1998: 58)

The 'Rights of Parents', in defining what parents can expect of a school
alongside what a school can expect of parents, reinforces the importance of
parents being part of the structure of the school, not just playing a part in it.
Cooperative understanding between parents and teachers brings value to
the educational prospects of the children, with the expectation that parents
will be active participants in the process (Malaguzzi 1997a: 215).

When discussing parental participation, educators in Reggio have
made the observation that 'families are interested in education, but
perhaps in a different way to educators' (Giacopini 2000). The school
recognises that it has a responsibility to demonstrate that parents' own
interpretation and understanding of their child, and of children in general, is valued and that it becomes part of the ongoing development of
the educational philosophy.

As Malaguzzi said, 'Parent participation enables a communication
network that leads to fuller and more reciprocal knowledge as well as
to a more effective search for the best educational methods, content and
values' (1997b: 215).

Parental participation

At the time a child enters an infant–toddler centre or preschool, the parents enter into a contract with that institution when they agree to be
active participants in the ongoing educational process (Cagliari *et al.*
2004: 28).

When children join the infant–toddler centres or preschools they
are welcomed through an induction programme. The programme is
planned to make the family feel at home and a part of the structure, and
to give educators the opportunity to talk with the parents and begin to

understand the parents' unique perspective on their own child. When children are about to start preschool, parents and children attend 'tea parties' where they have a glimpse of their new school. During the summer of their transition, the children take home a holiday bag or box which they then take to preschool with them the next term. This acts as a tangible 'thread of memory' for the child during the settling-in period and beyond (UK Study Tour 2000b). This settling-in process is complemented during the year by a series of class meetings, working groups, parties and outings. Class meetings involve teachers, parents and on occasion the atelierista, pedagogista and auxiliary staff, to discuss and compare ideas and knowledge about projects and issues of relevance to the class.

Each school has a prospectus, or 'identity note', which provides administrative information, sets out the philosophy of the school and includes a detailed floor plan of the layout of the building. In this way, parents are encouraged to become fully familiar with, and comfortable in their understanding of, the environment which their children inhabit. As a visitor to an infant–toddler centre or preschool, one is struck by the careful attention paid to the entrance area, described to us as the area where the school introduces and identifies itself. Here there is information about the school and the staff, a plan of the building and documentation of recent and past projects, all designed to make parents, children and visitors feel welcome (UK Study Tour 1999).

Documentation is used as a form of visual communication to nurture parents' interest and enable them to connect with the work of the schools. At the end of the afternoon in an infant–toddler centre, many of the parents arriving to collect their young children go straight to a book placed on a stand in the piazza near their children's classroom. In this book are photographs taken by staff capturing a significant event that has happened during the day. By looking at the book before entering the children's room, parents have a point of contact for subsequent conversation with their child and the member of staff responsible for them (UK Study Tour 2000b).

Early Childhood Council

As part of the management structure of each preschool and infant–toddler centre, there is an Early Childhood Council comprising elected representatives of the parents, staff and local community. As well as organising discussions on educational and cultural issues, various committees deal with the practical/functional aspects of the school, including external and internal maintenance of the building and the annual repainting of the furniture (UK Study Tour 2000a).

Periodically, inter-council meetings are held on themes of interest to a number of schools, providing broader opportunities for sharing of ideas. Since 1998, the Councils have collectively produced a parents' newsletter, *La Montgolfiera* ('The Hot Air Balloon'). This is used to encourage communication and participation and is distributed via all the early childhood institutions and associated organisations in Reggio Emilia.

Teachers

A collegiate, mutually supportive, approach is very evident within the philosophy and the organisational structure of the early childhood institutions. To the visitor it is obvious that all the adults in the structure are valued for the opportunities they provide for the children, and respect for the contribution made by the support staff is very visible.

In 'The Rights of Teachers' it is stated that:

> It is the right of the teachers and workers of each school to contribute to the study and preparation of the conceptual models that define the educational content, objectives and practices . . . through open discussion among the staff, with the pedagogical coordinators and the parent advisory committees . . .
>
> (Malaguzzi 1997a: 215)

Relationships between educators and parents are underpinned by a clear understanding of the rights (and duties) of parents to be fully involved in their children's education. Parents are valued in their own right by teachers, and as an additional source of expertise and experience. Again the three-year period that teachers spend with a particular group of children provides ample time for strong positive relationships to be established, underpinned by regular class meetings and activities.

During the settling-in process, staff do not make specific home visits, but an invitation to visit the homes of their pupils' families for tea or dinner is often accepted, as friends rather than as teachers (UK Study Tour 2000a). It is an annual tradition that children, educators and parents go to the countryside together at the time of the grape harvest (Malaguzzi 1997b: 105).

Team teaching, with two teachers working with a group of 26 children, provides opportunities for sharing ideas, supporting and in turn being supported by the process of documentation. Time exists for the establishment of strong relationships with these children as they progress through the school, supporting a deep understanding of their learning strategies. As part of their day-to-day work, teachers exchange information and observations of children in small and large groups to further their understanding of an individual child's learning. They are supported in this process by discussions with the atelierista and pedagogista with whom they review documentation and plan new opportunities.

Interdependence and the sharing of ideas and responsibility are viewed as strengths in Reggio, not weaknesses. Exchange of ideas is full and frank and requires a positive disposition towards constructive criticism (Gambetti 2001: 116; Rubizzi 2001: 94). A clearly-stated objective of this collegiate approach is that no parent, no child, no teacher and no specialist should ever feel on their own.

The teachers within the infant–toddler centres and preschools of Reggio Emilia regard themselves as being in a hugely privileged and responsible position. They see themselves as professionals who have a duty to respond to the changing world in order to best serve the needs of the children. As Carlina Rinaldi said:

> Teaching is a very old profession and one of great importance, value and responsibility. As teachers we have the privileged position and the duty to change the way we think and act, to reflect, to live our values in the world and to form better relationships on an individual and global level. We must have open minds in order to change as the world changes.
>
> (International Students and Professors Study Group 2006)

Environment and resources

The relationship between the people – adults and children – in Reggio and the environment they inhabit is the focus of much of the work of preschools and infant–toddler centres. Understanding of a 'sense of self' in relation to other people is extended to encompass an awareness of 'self' in relation to the environment one inhabits and the resources available for creative expression.

From a very young age, children are helped to see themselves as citizens of Reggio Emilia through projects which give them direct experience of the public buildings, parks, porticos and piazzas of the city (Bonilauri and Filippini 2000: 138).

In Reggio, the expression 'the environment as the third teacher' recognises the influence that physical space has on the children's development by either helping or hindering the learning process. Environments are constructed to encourage interaction and communication, creative expression, risky freedom and social responsibility, all supporting a collaborative, problem-solving approach to learning.

For historical as well as philosophical reasons, the use of natural and recycled materials has always been a feature of the work of the Reggio schools. Creative use of these resources not only produces some very striking visual images, but at the same time reinforces the wider social and global responsibilities of individuals as consumers.

Community

The relationship between the early childhood institutions and the city of Reggio Emilia has grown and developed over 60 years, particularly since the 1960s when the Municipality became involved in their funding and management. Community representatives are elected members of the Early Childhood Councils of each centre, and support for the complete range of services available to families is a funding priority for the Municipality of Reggio Emilia.

The preschools and infant–toddler centres see it as their responsibility to give back to the community that invests in them and to make their work, and their ideals and aspirations for young children, visible within the city and understood by all. Children become involved in large-scale projects, such as designing the safety curtain for the Ariosto Theatre (Vecchi 2002), compiling a guide to the city of Reggio as seen through their eyes (Davoli and Ferri 2000), and making known their thoughts and fears about war on huge banners attached to the columns of the Municipal Theatre (Piccinini 2002: 12).

The importance of the relationship between the early childhood institutions and the city of Reggio Emilia was described by Elena Giacopini, pedagogista: 'Education should occupy public spaces and not solely be within the walls of the institution. Reggio schools are set within the city and are visible to the city. The city of the children, the city for the children' (Giacopini 2000).

When the Loris Malaguzzi Centre was opened in 2006 as a central part of the regeneration programme in Reggio Emilia, a permanent installation *'Bicitante'* ('Bikes . . . Lots') was displayed in the pedestrian tunnel from the railway station to the Centre. This installation made public the project on the topic of the bicycle, carried out by children and students from the infant–toddler centres to the high school, creating a connectivity between the educational world and the general public (Cepi *et al.* 2014).

Recent changes in the population demographics of Reggio Emilia, with an influx of new residents from other areas of Italy and from different parts of the world, have stimulated an active debate on how best to learn from the experiences and values of different cultures. Out of this process of active involvement and sharing come new ideas, new possibilities and new ways forward. The schools in Reggio are constantly evolving, responding in a culturally appropriate way to the demands of a changing society. Change and uncertainty are seen as positive, and are welcomed as opportunities for new investigations, new organisational structures and new ways of working (Piccinini 2004: 5).

Key points

1. Reciprocal relationships are of fundamental importance – valuing each person's differences, skills and points of view.
2. Relationships are valued and supported through 'the pedagogy of listening'.
3. Relationships encompass not only people, but also the environment, resources, the community and the wider world.
4. The Charter of Rights sets out the rights and duties of children, teachers and parents.
5. The image of the child in Reggio is of 'a child that is rich in potential, strong and powerful'.
6. Parental participation lies at the heart of the pedagogical experience.
7. Documentation is used as a form of visible listening and as a means of fostering relationships with parents.
8. Teachers work within a collegiate structure in partnership with parents, children, the atelierista and the pedagogical team.

9. The environment – indoors and outdoors, natural and man-made – plays an integral role in young children's learning.
10. The reciprocal relationship between the early childhood institutions and the city of Reggio Emilia is highly valued and respected.

Reflections on the Reggio Approach

1. Relationships in your setting:
   - How much value do you place on reciprocal relationships in your setting?
   - Are children and parents respected and valued?
   - How do you demonstrate this?
2. Active listening:
   - How do you consult with the children and the other adults in your setting?
   - Do you consider other opinions and points of view?
   - Is time set aside for conversation and discussion?
3. Working together:
   - Is 'working together' valued in your setting?
   - Do you share observations and interpretations with colleagues on a regular basis?
   - How do you enable all members of staff to contribute?
4. Parental participation:
   - How do you make parents feel welcomed and valued?
   - What strategies do you use to share information with parents?
   - How do you encourage parents to be active partners in their children's learning?
5. Involving the community:
   - What value do you place on good relationships with your local community?
   - How do you make the work of your setting visible to the wider world?

Note

1. *Reggio Tutta: A Guide to the City by the Children* © Municipality of Reggio Emilia – Infant–Toddler Centres and Preschools, published by Reggio Children, Reggio Emilia, 2000, p. 76.

References

Bonilauri, S. and Filippini, T. (2000) 'The city: images, ideas and theories', in Davoli, M. and Ferri, G. (eds) *Reggio Tutta: A Guide to the City by the Children*, Reggio Children, Reggio Emilia, pp. 138–45.

Bruner, J. (2004) 'Reggio: a city of courtesy, curiosity and imagination', *Children in Europe*, 6, 27.

Cagliari, P., Barozzi, A. and Giudici, C. (2004) 'Thoughts, theories and experiences for an educational project with participation', *Children in Europe*, 6, 28–30.

Cepi, G., Deirio, G., Giacopini, E., Lambertson, O., Maffei, S., Massini, S., Montanari, R., Piazza, G., Prodi, R., Viale, G. *et al.* (2014) *Bikes. . .Lots!*, Reggio Children, Reggio Emilia.

Davoli, M. and Ferri, G. (eds) (2000) *Regio Tutta: A Guide to the City by the Children*, Reggio Children, Reggio Emilia.

Gambetti, A. (2001) 'Conversation with a group of teachers', in Giudici, C., Rinaldi, C. and Krechevsky, M. (eds) *Making Learning Visible: Children as Individual and Group Learners*, Reggio Children, Reggio Emilia, pp. 116–35.

Giacopini, E. (2000) 'Historical, cultural and pedagogical aspects of the Reggio Emilia municipal infant–toddler and preschool experience'. Presentation to UK Study Group, October, Reggio Emilia.

International Students and Professors Study Group (2006). Notes on Carlina Rinaldi's closing remarks.

Malaguzzi, L. (1997a) 'A Charter of Rights', in Filippini, T. and Vecchi, V. (eds) *The Hundred Languages of Children. Narrative of the Possible*, Reggio Children, Reggio Emilia, pp. 214–15.

Malaguzzi, L. (1997b) 'Harvesting grapes with the farmers', in Filippini, T. and Vecchi, V. (eds) *The Hundred Languages of Children. Narrative of the Possible*, Reggio Children, Reggio Emilia, pp. 104–5.

Malaguzzi, L. (1998) 'History, ideas and basic philosophy', in Edwards, C., Gandini, L. and Forman, G. (eds) *The Hundred Languages of Children: The Reggio Emilia Approach – Advanced Reflections* (2nd edn), Albex, Stamford, CT, pp. 49–97.

Piccinini, S. (2002) 'A city, its theatre, the children: an ongoing dialogue', in Vecchi, V. (ed.) *Theatre Curtain*, Reggio Children, Reggio Emilia.

Piccinini, S. (2004) 'A transforming city', *Children in Europe*, 6, 4–5.

Rinaldi, C. (1999a) 'The pedagogy of listening'. Presentation to UK Study Group, Reggio Emilia, spring.

Rinaldi, C. (1999b) 'Visible listening', *rechild*, 3, 7, Reggio Children.

Rinaldi, C. (2000) 'Visible listening'. Presentation to UK Study Group, October, Reggio Emilia.

Rinaldi, C. (2001) 'Documentation and assessment: what is the relationship?', in Giudici, C., Rinaldi, C. and Krechevsky, M. (eds) *Making Learning Visible: Children as Individual and Group Learners*, Reggio Children, Reggio Emilia, pp. 78–89.

Rinaldi, C. (2006) 'The child is the "first citizen"', in *Crossing Boundaries. Ideas and Experiences in Dialogue for a New Culture of Education and Adults* (edizioni junior), Reggio Children, Reggio Emilia, pp. 101–6.

Rubizzi, L. (2001) 'Documenting the documenter', in Giudici, C., Rinaldi, C. and Krechevsky, M. (eds) *Making Learning Visible: Children as Individual and Group Learners*, Reggio Children, Reggio Emilia, pp. 94–115.

Spaggiari, S. (1998) 'The community–teacher partnership in the governance of schools', in Edwards, C., Gandini, L. and Forman, G. (eds) *The Hundred Languages of Children. The Reggio Emilia Approach – Advanced Reflections* (2nd edn), Albex, Stamford, CT, pp. 99–112.

UK Study Tour (1999) Identity cards of the Alice infant–toddler centre and Diana preschool.

UK Study Tour (2000a) Notes from a visit to the Diana municipal preschool, October.

UK Study Tour (2000b) Notes from a visit to the Bellelli infant–toddler centre.

Vecchi, V. (2002) 'The courage of creativity', in Vecchi, V. (ed.) *Theatre Curtain*, Reggio Children, Reggio Emilia, p. 19.

5 | Time

The sea is born from the mother wave.
Time is born from the tempest.
The wind is born from the air and has the right shape to
**   bang things.**
Time is born from the years.[1]

It is an approach in which the importance of the unexpected and the possible
are recognised, an approach where there is no such thing as wasted time, but
in which teachers know how to give children all the time they need.

(Rinaldi 1998: 115)

This chapter describes the different ways in which time is valued and appreciated as a major contributor to the development of children's learning. The importance of time as continuity, time for day-to-day events and activities, and time for longer-term projects (*progettazione*) is discussed. The use of time on a daily basis is illustrated by descriptions of two 'typical days', one in an infant–toddler centre and the other in a preschool. Finally, the learning experiences gained during the process of one example of a long-term project are highlighted.

Previous chapters have explored the important contributions that the environment and relationships make to the pedagogical approach to early education of the Reggio preschools and infant–toddler centres. Crucial to a full understanding of the pedagogy and philosophy is an appreciation of the synergy that exists between space, relationships and time.

Time is valued for the continuity it gives children and adults as they live and grow together over extended periods of time. Time is valued within the day through the 'rich normality' of everyday experiences – time to meet, to be, to do, to think and reflect, to talk and listen, to rest and to eat. It is valued for the opportunities it provides for sustained long-term projects.

The approach of educators in Reggio to the management of time is described by Amelia Gambetti in her comments on a series of documentation panels from *The Hundred Languages of Children* exhibition. The panels, entitled 'Metaphors and Scripts: The Intimacy of Wire' showed 2-year-old children experiencing and investigating wire.

> The time the children work can be short, or it can be long. The strong statement is that children have time – time to stay there, to go back and forth, to return and see things from a different point of view. Something like this can happen in a very short time, but there will have been many other times that have made it possible.
>
> (Gambetti 2003: 76)

Time as continuity

Educators and parents share an understanding that children will be a part of the infant–toddler or preschool structure for several years. There is no sense of urgency to push their education on and prepare them for the next stage. Children have time to fully experience the joy of being 1, or 3, or 5 years old, and educators have time to tune in to and respect the rhythm of children's learning. Over time a 'portrait of the child' emerges, visualising the child as a whole and the child in relation to others. When children transfer from the infant–toddler centre to preschool, this portfolio of information is collected together to create a 'Book of Passage' detailing their skills and competencies (UK Study Tour 2000a).

Many of the long-term projects that have been carried out are linked and build on one another. For example, the project 'Catness' started when a cat, attracted to the preschool garden by visitors to the Amusement Park for Birds, gave birth to a litter of kittens (Piazza 1999), and the project 'Theatre Curtain' built on children's experiences of the city as described in *Reggio Tutta: A Guide to the City by the Children* (Piccinini 2002: 12). The documentation from projects which have happened in the past is part of the identity of the individual preschools and infant–toddler centres and remains there as a reminder of the importance of being aware of the present, but at the same time building on the past and looking to the future (Spaggiari 2004).

Reflection and recollection are day-to-day activities for children in Reggio. A project from the Diana School, building specifically on this process, involved a class of 5- and 6-year-old children compiling their own version of the school prospectus for the 3-year-olds due to start in September. This child's eye view of life in a Reggio preschool gives a profound insight into the Reggio experience in the words and thoughts of the chief protagonists, the children. It is also extremely honest and amusing (Strozzi and Vecchi 2002).

Time for day-to-day experiences

The rationale behind the structure of a typical day is best described in the words of Paola Strozzi, a teacher in the Diana School: 'Once an overall time frame has been set (9.00 for arrival, 12.00 for lunch, 3.30 for snack and 4.00 or 6.30 for departure), what determines the beginning or end of an activity is primarily the children's interests and desires' (Strozzi 2001: 74).

The following two sections illustrate a 'typical day' in an infant–toddler centre and a preschool.

A day in the life of a 'virtual toddler' in Toddlers 1 (10–18 months)

Arrival: 7.30–9.00 am

The moment of arrival is seen as 'a hinge between the two delicate worlds' of home and the centre. As children arrive and are greeted, teachers enter into dialogue with both the child and the parents based around that morning's experiences from home. The moment of saying goodbye is a respected and delicate time, valued for the effect it will have on both parent and child for the rest of the day.

Children often bring things of interest from home – these precious objects are given great value and are interwoven into the activities of the day. The rhythm of everyday life continues through play, investigation, interaction and exploration.

Morning: 9.00 am

Most of the children attend Monday to Friday over a period of 2 to 3 years. There is time to spend together to build relationships, skills and competencies. Educators feel no pressure to push or accelerate children's development but recognise the importance of growing and constructing meanings over time.

The children are divided into small groups to pursue different activities that attract their interest. For example, the children will be working with mirrors, playing in the construction area, using clay, looking at books and playing peek-a-boo with the birds through the windows. Some children help the cook to prepare snacks and lunch.

Lunchtime: 11.00 am

All of the children meet in the dining room for lunch. The teachers and kitchen staff sit with the children during the meal, but have their own lunch later in the day.

Preparation for sleep: 12.00 noon

Some children leave after lunch and the remainder prepare for sleep. This is a time to play with light and dark, experimenting with torches and lights in different places to create the right atmosphere for sleep.

Afternoon sleep and quiet play: 1.00 pm

When the children are sleeping and playing the teachers have lunch and meet to discuss and reflect on the morning's activities and plan for the following days.

Afternoon snack: 2.45 pm

Preparation for departure: 3.00–3.30 pm

A time for coming back together, talking about the day and telling stories. A time for children to recognise and appreciate, along with others, the rhythm of the day.

Departure: 4.00–6.20 pm

Parents, grandparents and carers arrive to collect the children – the delicate moment of departure. There is a feeling of 'until tomorrow' nurtured by the sharing of information between the adults. Opportunities are provided for parents to establish a point of contact with their children's experiences during the day through photographs, notes or short transcripts of the words they have spoken.

(UK Study Tour 2000a)

The daily schedule of an infant–toddler centre

7.30–9.00 am	arrival
11.00 am	lunch
12.00–12.45 pm	preparation for nap time and midday departure
12.45 pm	afternoon nap
2.45 pm	snack
3.30–4.00 pm	departure
4.00–6.20 pm	extended day

A day in the life of the 4- and 5-year-olds in a preschool

The school that awaits

7.30 am – The school awaits the children, parents and staff. It greets them with the early morning light, which filters through the large windows and from the two inner courtyards. In this environment the natural light dialogues with the colours and surfaces, and transparency underlines the relationship and exchange of information between the inside and the outside: the season, the weather and the light at different times of day. The physical environment is inviting. Its furnishings suggest to the children and their parents stories to be created or continued.

(Strozzi 2001: 61)

Arrival: 7.30–9.00 am

A few children and parents arrive at 7.30 am and are welcomed by one of the teachers into the classroom nearest the door. The act of welcoming is an important event. It is a time for re-establishing relationships in an environment where children and adults spend a significant portion of their lives together. The children eagerly await the arrival of their friends to exchange news and ideas and have animated discussions about possibilities for the coming day. They organise themselves into groups, often involving children of different ages, and engage in activities such as playing board games, writing stories and imaginary play.

The first of the class teachers arrives at 8.00 am and begins to review her notes for the proposed projects for the day, based on monthly and weekly forecasts. Some children join in and express their opinions about what might happen and help the teacher to prepare the resources that might be needed.

At 8.30 am the second teacher arrives and is greeted by a group of children. The co-teachers, sometimes with the involvement of the atelierista, use these precious moments to ask for advice, exchange information and make adjustments to their plans for the day based on the previous day's work and the ideas suggested by the children that morning.

Morning session: 9.00–11.30 am

When all of the children have arrived, the early morning activities are tidied away and the class comes together as a large group. This assembly of children and adults will share fruit, talk about personal events and decide together how to spend the morning. They discuss ideas, find agreement, decide on groups and where they will work. Some children need more time to decide what they want to do. They need to peer and watch what others are doing. Wandering is not seen as an 'absence of mind', but rather a strategy of waiting before choosing their investigations (Davoli 2004). Not all activities will be new ones, some will have begun days or weeks earlier. Children are encouraged and expected to concentrate for extended periods of time to deepen their levels of involvement and understanding.

Children move to other parts of the school, inside and outside, with the agreement of the teacher.

Reflection: 11.30–12.00 noon

The large group reconvenes to talk and reflect on the morning. This is a time to focus on new questions which have arisen, the successes, challenges and difficulties of the morning and to evaluate what remains unfinished. Some children clear away and others prepare the room for rest, reading or listening to music.

Lunch: 12.00 noon

The children set their own places for lunch next to their 'friend of the day'. Time spent around the lunch table is culturally important and emphasises the sense of belonging to a group.

Afternoon session: 1.00–3.00 pm

Many children will have a nap in the afternoon. One teacher remains with the children during the rest period and the others have lunch, discuss the events of the day and prepare any necessary notes for parents. Some children do not sleep for long. They respect the fact that their friends are sleeping and play games quietly, look at books and listen to music.

Snack time: 3.00 pm

The children have an afternoon snack and share new ideas and new stories for the next day.

Departure: 3.30–6.20 pm

Parents and carers arrive to collect the children and share a moment of communication about the activities of the day.

(Crossing Boundaries 2004a)

The daily schedule of a preschool

7.30–9.00 am	children arrive
9.00 am	play and organised work activities in large and small groups
12.00 noon	lunch
1.00 pm	afternoon nap
3.00 pm	snack in the classroom
3.30–4.00 pm	children leave
4.00–6.20 pm	extended day

Time for projects

Short- and long-term projects define the educational experience and provide the opportunity for teachers to learn alongside one another and alongside children. These projects, *progettazione*, may last only a matter of weeks, others continue for 4 to 6 months. Occasionally very long-term projects, such as the children's relationship with the city, described in *Reggio Tutta*, involve all the infant–toddler centres and preschools and last for up to 2 years (Davoli and Ferri 2000).

The word *progettazione* is derived from the Italian verb *progettare*, meaning to plan, to devise, or to project in a technical engineering sense. Used in an educational sense, this is seen to be in opposition to the word *programmazione* which implies a predefined curriculum. The concept of *progettazione* implies a flexible approach in which initial hypotheses are made about the work of the centres but which are subject to modifications and changes of direction as the work progresses (Gandini 2005).

The year does not start with a blank sheet; the educators have many years of experience of this way of working to draw upon (Malaguzzi 1998: 88). All the documentation gathered over the years will be available to the staff as part of the history of the school as well as forming part of their own professional development. Projects carried out many years ago can act as an inspiration for new projects and new investigations – a proposition or starting point put to a group of children several years ago may be re-presented to a new group of children to see what new ideas and theories emerge and what new lines of enquiry are opened.

In describing the process by which projects in a preschool are agreed, the pedagogista at the Diana School gave the following explanation:

At the beginning of the school year proposals for long-term projects arise from group discussion between children and teachers. These ideas are shared with the rest of the school and with the pedagogista – some will become projects and some not. By the end of October they are crystallised into a 'Declaration of Intent' which sets out the proposals for the coming year.

(UK Study Tour 2000b)

As a project develops, it may occasionally change course, go off at a tangent, and become a completely different project. Interest in insects and bugs in the garden led to a project involving a group of 5-year-old children beginning to construct an 'insect farm' in a small outside area next to the mini-atelier. The area was chosen so that it was clearly visible from the inside of the building so that children could view it four or five times a day and make a note of the insects they could see. The children then discovered an unexpected problem: 'How could they create a chart which represents the different periods of the day which would be understandable to the other children in the class, and to younger children in the school?' Discussion then centred on an exploration of symbols as a way of communicating information, and the original purpose of the project was forgotten – there was an agreement between the adults and the children that, at this time, the exploration of symbolic representation was far more important (Crossing Boundaries 2004b).

'Theatre Curtain' – the ring of transformations

This project, which started in March and ended in June 1999, was described by Vea Vecchi, the atelierista from the Diana School during the October 2000 UK Study Tour (Vecchi 2000). The full description, beautifully illustrated, is available in the publication *Theatre Curtain* (Vecchi 2002).

The project arose from a suggestion made by the theatre administrator that the children would like to create a curtain for the Municipal Theatre. The curtain would be large, functional, beautiful and visible to large numbers of people. After some initial concerns about the enormity of the task, the idea took root and the challenge was taken up by the educators.

A theatre curtain designed by preschool children?

This was certainly possible in Reggio Emilia, a city which has long given credit to children. But it could also happen in any city, anywhere in the world, that recognises that children have and construct their own cultures, that knows how to listen to their creativity and strength and that gives space not just to the usual and habitual.

(Piccinini 2002: 12)

Without disclosing the proposal to the children, arrangements were made to extend the children's experience of the theatre buildings. Groups of children visited the theatre building over a period of 10 days and explored it in detail, outside and inside. The children drew the outside of the building from many different angles and explored the spaces physically. They experienced the inside of the building using all their senses: looking, listening, touching, smelling and wondering.

While looking at and talking about the existing curtain, the atelierista put forward the proposal that the children should make a new curtain. The children were stunned by the proposal: 'I don't think we could do it because it would take too long, at least 11 days' (Federica); 'But if we all do something . . .' (Giulia).

The possibility of cooperation and teamwork reassured the children and they decided to go ahead.

The idea to use dragonflies, grasshoppers, plants and leaves arose from the children's interest in insects at this particular time of year (spring), and from their interest in the film *A Bug's Life* stickers which were popular at the time. The children used different methods for their drawings: life drawing, looking at photographs, and their imagination. The unifying criterion was that the plants and animals should look alive.

Out of the children's discussions about their drawings came an observation about transformations – how adding an eye to a leaf can transform it into something else. The children became fascinated by the concept of transformation and this then became the guiding theme for the project. 'Transformation and metamorphosis are processes that lie somewhere between biology and magic' (Vecchi 2002: 65).

Over the next few weeks the children experimented with fine-line drawings and graphic designs which could transform from one thing to another. Each child in the class chose one of their drawings that they felt would be most appropriate for the curtain, and these were scanned to create digital images.

The challenge now was to put together the final composition from the individual drawings. To do this, the children needed to spend time becoming familiar with the technology they were going to use and the potential it provided for altering digital images. In groups of two or three, the children chose the images they wished to use, enlarged them on the photocopier and composed them in a collage form. Glue was only used when the most suitable composition had been decided upon.

Now came a difficult time in the life of the project. For 2 weeks the project stalled with no obvious route forward. Following discussion, the teachers decided to propose to the children the idea of creating collective stories by moving the drawings around on a sheet of paper before creating gigantic enlargements of the patterns.

Up until now, all the children in the class had been involved in the project. From experience of other large-scale projects, the teachers decided to identify a smaller group of children to take the project forward. They did this to eliminate the danger of the teachers making the decisions and the children merely carrying them out. The group was identified by the interest shown in the project, the children's competencies and group dynamics. Four girls and three boys formed the working group for the final design.

The boys carried out one design and the girls another, retaining the themes of transformation and narration. Now there were two designs, but only one curtain. The children discussed and negotiated and finally agreed on the boys' design as the one which would be recreated. At the end of the morning session, the two choices for the final design and the discussions about them were reported to the whole class, who approved the final choice.

A photocopier was used to produce the next phase of the design at a quarter of the final size. This was too big to be worked on in the school so the work now continued in the painters' loft in the Municipal Theatre. For the next 20 days, three or four children, accompanied by two adults, worked on the project at the theatre, painting the image onto a sheet of clear plastic. From time to time the teacher suggested to the children that they pause, step back, evaluate the painting and agree on how to proceed. 'The more the work progresses, the greater the children's awareness and engagement become as they reflect on what they have done, make choices, and ask for and give opinions' (Vecchi 2002: 102).

Finally, the painting was finished – all the children in the class visited the painters' loft and toasted the success of the project with orange soda. Months of thought, imagination, challenge, cooperation and resilience came to fruition in a spectacular example of children's creative learning which was celebrated at an official opening ceremony in the Ariosto Theatre in March 2000 (Spaggiari 2002: 9; Vecchi 2000).

This example of a long-term project illustrates the value of:

- trusting the children to come up with good ideas;
- building on a good understanding of individual children's dispositions, skills, interests and attitudes;
- allowing all the children to engage in multi-sensory exploration;
- choosing the appropriate moment to propose the initial idea for the project;
- helping the children to learn new skills and competencies to enable them to fulfil a brief;
- recording and reflecting on all the learning that is taking place;
- developing strategies to cope with uncertainty;
- celebrating success.

Educators in Reggio Emilia, and indeed the whole administrative structure of the city, have a keen appreciation of their place in the time continuum. They combine an understanding of the past with an awareness of the present and a sense of responsibility to look to the future with hope and optimism (Spaggiari 2004).

Key points

1. Great value is placed on giving children the time they need to explore and develop their ideas and theories.
2. The period from birth to age 6 years is valued as a phase in its own right, and as part of the continuum of children's learning and development.
3. Children are encouraged to be aware of the present, build on the past, and look to the future.
4. Time for talking, reflecting and sharing ideas is valued and respected.
5. The potential learning opportunities inherent in day-to-day activities are recognised and exploited.
6. The rhythm of the day is broken only by fixed points such as arrival, lunch and departure.

7. From a very young age, children are encouraged, and expected, to concentrate for long periods of time.
8. Children manage their own time, and are able to leave unfinished investigations knowing that they can return to them later.
9. Time is valued for the opportunities it provides for long-term projects, some of which will last several months.
10. The Reggio Approach is the product of over 40 years of observation, interpretation, discussion and research.

Reflections on the Reggio Approach

1. Continuity:
   - Are 'traces of the past' evident within your setting?
   - Do you use these as starting points for new ideas and explorations?
   - Are children actively encouraged to remember, and develop, a 'sense of history'?
2. Rhythm of the day:
   - How is the pattern of the day determined in your setting?
   - What are the fixed points in the day?
   - Could changes be made to allow children more uninterrupted time during the course of the day?
3. Time to talk and reflect:
   - Is time for talk and discussion valued? How do you demonstrate this?
   - Do children have time to reflect on what they have done during the day?
   - Do staff make time to reflect on and discuss what they have been involved in during the course of the day/week?
4. Long-term projects:
   - How do you make time for the development of longer-term projects and extended play themes?
   - Are time and space set aside for children to return to 'work in hand'?
   - How do you encourage children to manage their own time?
5. Smooth transitions:
   - How do you build up a 'portrait of the child' when they first join your setting?

- What evidence of children's development and learning – skills, dispositions, attitudes and feelings – do you collect during the time they spend with you?
- How do you share this information with parents and with the setting the child will move on to?

Note

1. *The Hundred Languages of Children: Catalogue of the Exhibition* © Municipality of Reggio Emilia – Infant–Toddler Centres and Preschools, published by Reggio Children, Reggio Emilia, 1996, p. 203.

References

Crossing Boundaries (2004a) 'The right to environment. Children, spaces, relations. Pedagogy and architecture'. Seminar at Crossing Boundaries International Conference, February, Reggio Emilia.

Crossing Boundaries (2004b) Visit to Michelangelo municipal preschool, Crossing Boundaries International Conference, February, Reggio Emilia.

Davoli, A. (2004) Crossing Boundaries International Conference, February, Reggio Emilia.

Davoli, M. and Ferri, G. (2000) *Reggio Tutta: A Guide to the City by the Children*, Reggio Children, Reggio Emilia.

Gambetti, A. (2003) 'Teachers living in collaboration', in Cadwell, L. B. *Bringing Learning to Life. The Reggio Approach to Early Childhood Education*, Teachers College Press, Columbia University, New York and London, pp. 67–100.

Gandini, L. (2005) 'Glossary', in *In the Spirit of the Studio-Learning from the Atelier of Reggio Emilia*, Teachers College Press, Columbia University, New York and London, p. 98.

Malaguzzi, L. (1998) 'History, ideas and basic philosophy', in Edwards, C., Gandini, L. and Forman, G. (eds) *The Hundred Languages of Children: The Reggio Emilia Approach – Advanced Reflections* (2nd edn), Albex, Stamford, CT, pp. 49–97.

Piazza, G. (1999) 'Catness'. Seminar presentation to UK Study Group.

Piccinini, S. (2002) 'The city, its theatre, the children: an ongoing dialogue', in Vecchi, V. (ed.) *Theatre Curtain*, Reggio Children, Reggio Emilia, pp. 12–13.

Rinaldi, C. (1998) 'Projected curriculum construction through documentation – progettazione', in Edwards, C., Gandini, L. and Forman, G. (eds) *The Hundred Languages of Children: The Reggio Emilia Approach – Advanced Reflections* (2nd edn), Albex, Stamford, CT.

Spaggiari, A. (2002) 'A precious work', in Vecchi, V. (ed.) *Theatre Curtain*, Reggio Children, Reggio Emilia, pp. 8–9.

Spaggiari, A. (2004) Opening address at Crossing Boundaries International Conference, February, Reggio Emilia.

Strozzi, P. (2001) 'Daily life at school: seeing the extraordinary in the ordinary', in Giudici, C., Rinaldi, C. and Krechevsky, M., *Making Learning Visible: Children as Individual and Group Learners*, Reggio Children, Reggio Emilia, pp. 58–77.

Strozzi, P. and Vecchi, V. (eds) (2002) *Advisories*, Reggio Children, Reggio Emilia.

UK Study Tour (2000a) Notes from visit to the Bellelli infant–toddler centre.

UK Study Tour (2000b) Notes from visit to the Diana municipal preschool.

Vecchi, V. (2000) 'The curtain of the Ariosto Theatre'. Seminar presentation to UK Study Group, October.

Vecchi, V. (ed.) (2002) *Theatre Curtain*, Reggio Children, Reggio Emilia.

Children and teachers as researchers: individual and group learning

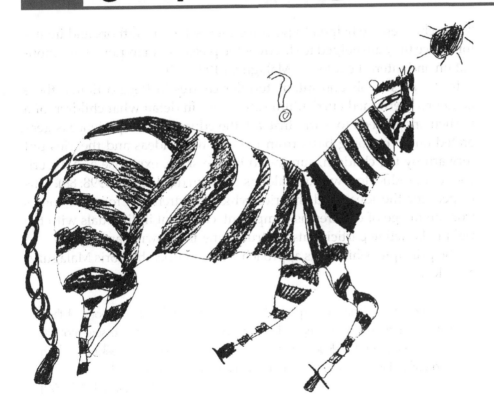

Andrea and Elisa F. – In the shadow of a zebra, can you see the white stripes or the black stripes better?[1]

For children to be in a group is a situation of great privilege, as if inside a great, transforming laboratory.

(Malaguzzi 1998: 95)

This chapter reviews the concept of children and teachers as researchers and the ways in which research is viewed as an ordinary, everyday process rather than a specialised activity. The principles that underpin group learning are discussed, and the use of large, medium and small group arrangements are illustrated with reference to a group of preschool-age children. Finally, the collaborative research into group and individual learning being carried out by educators in Italy and the USA is introduced.

Children as researchers

'Once children are helped to perceive themselves as authors and inventors, once they are helped to discover the pleasures of inquiry, their motivation and interest explode' (Malaguzzi 1998: 67).

In the preschools and infant–toddler centres in Reggio Emilia there is no predetermined curriculum setting out in detail what children of a particular age need to learn. Instead, the educational experience is generated on an ongoing basis from the questions, ideas and theories put forward by the children, supported by the skills, expertise and experience of the educators working alongside them (Malaguzzi 1998: 88). This respect for the ideas and theories which children put forward comes from an image of children as competent, confident individuals with the right to be active participants in structuring their own learning.

The principle behind this approach was described by Loris Malaguzzi as follows:

> Our intention is clearly to help children search for and discover parts of their world that may risk remaining hidden. Moreover we want to be sure that the desires, interests and intelligences, and capacity for enjoying and seeking – which are a child's inborn resources – do not remain buried and unused.
>
> (Malaguzzi 1997: 62)

Evidence from the educational research project which has been ongoing in Reggio for many years has shown that children, in their search to make sense of the world around them, can be trusted to 'ask the important questions' (Rinaldi 2002). These questions then become the starting points for further investigation and exploration. Some will lead to longer-term projects, or *progettazione*, which may be developed over the course of several months. The concept of *progettazione* is based on the belief that knowledge building is neither linear nor predetermined, that the development of knowledge is a group process, and that children produce their own theories and hold their own values. Fundamental to the notion of *progettazione* is the value of research as a mode of learning, leading towards 'the unknown result' (Rinaldi 2007).

During the development of a project, children's theories are developed through focused discussion among children and adults. The children are encouraged to express their ideas graphically in pictures and drawings and then to use these images to explain their ideas to the rest of the group. When a child represents his mental images to others he is also 're-presenting' them to himself, developing his awareness of symbolic language, modifying his theory and deepening his understanding (Malaguzzi 1998: 92). With sensitive guidance from the teacher, children with similar theories are encouraged to 'relaunch' their ideas cooperatively and to develop them through ongoing discussion, drawing, 3-D representation and re-enactment.

To facilitate this process, children make use of the wide range of tools and resources which are available to them in the atelier. The atelier of each school contains a core range of resources supplemented by more sophisticated equipment which reflects the interests and expertise of the atelierista in the school. This could include musical instruments and related technology, a binocular microscope linked to a display screen, or ICT equipment, including digital cameras, computers and scanners.

The role of adults in supporting children as researchers is to provide interesting resources and experiences, or provocations, which engage the children's attention and prompt further exploration and investigation. They also act as a resource with knowledge, skills and expertise that children can access as required.

Teachers as researchers

The role of the teacher in Reggio is not to teach, but to learn. Teachers are viewed as researchers, constantly evaluating and reflecting on their interactions with the children. In a discussion with Peter Moss and Gunilla Dahlberg on becoming a competent teacher, Carlina Rinaldi states:

> What I try to do with students is to help them encounter their own image of the child, to reflect on it, understand the implications for education of the image of the child they have – in terms of values, strategies, the quality of relationship with children and so on.
>
> (Rinaldi 2006: 194)

Teachers are expected to be competent, well informed and intellectually curious, and to take responsibility for managing their own professional development (Rinaldi 1994: 49). Their aim as teachers is to develop their own understanding of how children learn, and how group dynamics operate, in order to provide more meaningful learning situations. Time is available during the working day for teachers to share ideas, thoughts and observations, and weekly meetings with the rest of the school staff and the pedagogista are occasions to reflect on past experiences and plan future opportunities.

In Reggio, research is not regarded as an activity which occurs solely in academic institutions and university departments. Instead the educators speak of the 'normality of research' and regard it as part of the day-to-day life of the preschools and infant–toddler centres (Rinaldi 2002).

This demands of the adults an approach to life which values the unknown and welcomes doubt and uncertainty. In the words of Carlina Rinaldi:

> Children can give us the strength of doubt and the courage of error. They can transmit to us the joy of searching and researching . . . the value of research, as an openness towards others and toward everything new that is produced by encounter with others.
>
> (Rinaldi 2003: 2)

This research-based approach keeps the educational experience of Reggio ever changing and evolving, creating an environment in which educators continue to work with enthusiasm for many years. From the outset, Malaguzzi defined their aim as follows:

> We wanted to recognise the right of each child to be a protagonist and the need to sustain each child's spontaneous curiosity at a high level. We had to preserve our decision to learn from events, and from the families to the full extent of our professional limits, and to maintain a readiness to change points of view so as never to have too many certainties.
>
> (Malaguzzi 1998: 52)

Group learning

The strong emphasis on relationships that underpins many different aspects of the Reggio Approach recognises the link which exists between social interaction and cognitive development. Children have a right to be connected to others and to have their sense of identity reinforced through interaction with their peers and with adults. Relationships are fostered through children staying together as a class for the whole time they spend in an infant–toddler centre or preschool.

Organisational structures focus on groups of learners rather than individuals. The importance of group learning has as its philosophical base the belief that multiple perspectives, of other children and of adults, add value to the learning of the individual and that collegiality, cooperation and teamwork are vital skills for life.

In the group situation, children use each other's knowledge and experience to solve challenging problems and to extend their own understanding. Teachers respect the individuality of a child within a group, and plan from a clear understanding of where each child's research is going through the language they use and the cognitive skills they demonstrate. Group learning is valued for the many opportunities it provides for developing the skills of listening, expressing ideas, negotiating, resolving conflict and problem-solving. It is supported on a daily basis by the setting aside of time for discussion and debate, by organising space to facilitate interaction, and by the presence of two or more members of staff.

Group organisation in a preschool

During the course of the day, children move between collective (26 children), medium-sized (10–12 children) and small (2–4 children) groups, depending on the activity they are involved in. All these different group arrangements are important as each serves its own particular purpose.

At the start of the day, when all the children have arrived, there is a class assembly time, the first collective moment of the day. This has been described as: 'A time to gather, to reflect and to plan. It is a democratic moment, a circular parliament and a time for building relationships. It is an important contextual moment when children learn about all the proposals for the day' (UK Study Tour 2000a).

During this time the first small groups for the day are formed. There is no single criterion for group formation; sometimes it could be a friendship group proposed by a child, at other times a group of children with similar interests might be invited by the adult to work together, or the group might form to continue an activity that has already been started.

On a typical day, a small group of children will then move out of the main classroom into the mini-atelier, often accompanied by one of the class teachers, to continue their investigations. The remainder of the class works in groups on the activities they have chosen, supported by the second teacher. By agreement with the teacher the children are able to move around the school and choose where they want to be – the piazza, the atelier or the inner courtyard (UK Study Tour 2000b).

Group organisation in the 5-year-old children's classroom during a morning session

Two children, both girls, are working on a project on foil to improve the aesthetics of a design.

Four children are in the message area composing replies to a letter from a teacher from Boston, USA. They have a strong desire to communicate. They first dictate their message to a teacher but then want to create a final copy in their own writing.

Two children are using the computer to write. They have different levels of competency and share skills and knowledge as they work cooperatively.

In the atelier, six children are building, painting and creating animals with clay. This is part of a long-term project focusing on representing grasshoppers and lizards.

Three children are in the construction area using artificial light and recycled materials to create imaginary landscapes and scenes.

A cloud made of wire is being built by four children in the mini-atelier. This is part of a bigger project, involving all of the children, which will give everyone a chance to make a personal contribution to a construction designed to improve the atelier.

Music for the cloud is being composed by three children, who then decide to record a soundtrack.

The final two girls spend about 40 minutes wandering and peering before they find a place to settle. The light boxes capture their attention and they decide to paint the perfumes of a bunch of flowers. Throughout the morning other children gather to observe as they are interested to see how the work progresses.

The environment is consumed by light and the girls are using all of their senses to observe the perfumes. Maybe the perfumes they have painted can be smelled?

After a while the six children using clay decide to leave the atelier and migrate to other areas. Some move to the piazza and others go to see the 3-year-olds and offer their mentoring skills to the teachers of the younger children.

At the end of the morning session the class comes back together as a collective group, and ideas, theories and investigations are shared. Children have the opportunity to talk about their discoveries within the larger group so that children who are not directly involved in a particular activity have the opportunity to share in the experience and stay connected with it.

(Crossing Boundaries 2004)

An example of group learning – maps of the city of Reggio Emilia

Defining the best group arrangement for a particular purpose relies on the in-depth understanding the teachers have of the individual children in their class, their learning styles and the expressive languages they use. Observing how different groups of children approach an identical problem or task provides an insight into the influence gender, social and cultural factors can have on children's learning.

In the project entitled 'The City of Reggio Emilia' there are two examples of complex and detailed maps of the city drawn by two different groups of 5-year-old children, one a group of girls and the other a group of boys. These two groups had been deliberately divided by gender as part of ongoing research by the atelierista and the teacher.

The three girls formed a close cooperative group in which talk, often humorous, preceded action. They selected points of personal significance within the city and made social connections between them. The emphasis on parks, play areas and the main shopping street resulted in a map depicting a 'city of relationships'.

In the initial stages, two of the three boys worked together with the third observing. He was later drawn into the group by his peers. Conversation was almost absent as the boys drew a plan of the city starting from its piazzas. They then focused on the transport connections and services – the roads, railway, telegraph wires and drainage systems. Their map was one of a 'functioning city' (UK Study Tour 2000c; Piazza and Barozzi 2001).

Defining the learning group

The subject of group learning and the influence it has on the ongoing learning of the individuals that make up the group has itself been the subject of a long-term collaborative research project between Reggio Children and Project Zero at Harvard University (Giudici *et al.* 2001).

In discussing the findings of this research, Steve Seidel of Project Zero defined a learning group as: 'A collection of persons who are emotionally, intellectually and aesthetically engaged in solving problems, creating products and making meaning. A group in which each person learns autonomously and through the ways of learning of others' (Seidel 2002).

In Reggio, the concept of group learning has been developed in a particular way to support the philosophy and the pedagogy. The Project Zero research has identified four characteristic features of a learning group in Reggio. The group:

- includes adults as well as children;
- uses documentation of children's learning processes to make their learning visible as well as helping to shape the learning which is taking place;
- values the emotional and aesthetic elements of learning as much as the intellectual dimensions;
- recognises that the focus of learning extends beyond the learning of individuals to create a collective body of knowledge.
                    (Seidel 2002; Krechevsky and Mardell 2001: 284)

Making Learning Visible: Children as Individual and Group Learners (Giudici *et al.* 2001) gives a detailed and fascinating insight into the principles, organisation and management of the educational process in the infant–toddler centres and preschools of Reggio Emilia. Drawing on research from educators in Reggio and the USA, it provides different perspectives on the connections between group and individual learning and on the role of documentation in capturing the learning process.

Key points

1. Children's ideas, interests and theories are the starting point for developing the ongoing educational experience.
2. Evidence, gathered over many years, shows that children can be trusted to 'ask the important questions'.
3. Children are confident to suggest theories and take risks with their ideas, knowing that what they say will be respected and valued.
4. Discussion, graphical representation and 3-D modelling help children to refine their ideas and deepen their understanding.
5. Adults act as a resource of knowledge, skills and expertise which can be accessed by the children.
6. Teachers are learners, alongside the children.
7. Research is regarded as part of day-to-day life and not a specialised activity.
8. Group learning is highly valued, and children are encouraged to use the skills, knowledge and experience of their peers to extend their own understanding.
9. Group size and composition varies, each having its own particular purpose.
10. Documentation provides a means of capturing the processes of individual and group learning.

Reflections on the Reggio Approach

1. Image of the child:
   ■ How comfortable are you with the notion of children and adults as co-constructors of knowledge?
   ■ How do you support children as researchers?
   ■ Which 'languages of expression' do you value?
2. Asking good questions, having good conversations:
   ■ Have you tried observing how the adults in your setting ask questions and hold conversations with children?
   ■ Are questions often open-ended, to encourage discussion and investigation?
   ■ What opportunities do you provide for valuing the questions children ask and the theories they suggest?
3. Practitioners as researchers:
   ■ Does your working environment encourage intellectual curiosity and an eagerness to learn?

- How do you support action research in your setting?
- Do you provide an environment in which children and adults are confident to 'take risks' with their ideas?
4. Learning groups:
   - Do you value group learning as well as individual learning?
   - Do you provide a variety of different opportunities for children to learn together?
   - How do you support the development of skills and dispositions needed to be part of a learning group?
5. Learning styles:
   - How easy do you find it to recognise the different learning styles which children and adults use?
   - How do you ensure that you provide opportunities for children with different learning styles?
   - How do you find opportunities for children to use their many 'languages of expression'?

Note

1. *Everything Has a Shadow Except Ants* © Municipality of Reggio Emilia – Infant–Toddler Centres and Preschools, published by Reggio Children, Reggio Emilia, 1999, p. 89.

References

Crossing Boundaries (2004) 'The right to environment: Children, spaces, relations. Pedagogy and architecture'. Seminar at Crossing Boundaries International Conference, February, Reggio Emilia.

Giudici, C., Rinaldi, C. and Krechevsky, M. (eds) (2001) *Making Learning Visible: Children as Individual and Group Learners*, Reggio Children, Reggio Emilia.

Krechevsky, M. and Mardell, B. (2001) 'Four features of learning in groups', in Giudici, C., Rinaldi, C. and Krechevsky, M. (eds) *Making Learning Visible: Children as Individual and Group Learners*, Reggio Children, Reggio Emilia, pp. 284–94.

Malaguzzi, L. (1997) 'A heresy of light and colour', in Filippini, T. and Vecchi, V. (eds) *The Hundred Languages of Children. Narrative of the Possible*, Reggio Children, Reggio Emilia, p. 62.

Malaguzzi, L. (1998) 'History, ideas and basic philosophy', in Edwards, C., Gandini, L. and Forman, G. (eds) *The Hundred Languages of Children: the Reggio Emilia Approach – Advanced Reflections* (2nd edn), Albex, Stamford, CT, pp. 49–97.

Piazza, G. and Barozzi, A. (2001) 'The city of Reggio Emilia', in Giudici, C., Rinaldi, C. and Krechevsky, M. (eds) *Making Learning Visible: Children as Individual and Group Learners*, Reggio Children, Reggio Emilia, pp. 228–45.

Rinaldi, C. (1994) 'Staff development in Reggio Emilia', in Katz, L. G. and Cesarone, B. (eds) *Reflections on the Reggio Emilia Approach: Perspectives from ERIC/EECE*, University of Illinois, pp. 47–50.

Rinaldi, C. (2002) 'Teachers as researchers'. Presentation at ReFocus One Symposium, June, Kendal, UK.

Rinaldi, C. (2003) 'The teacher as researcher', *Innovations* (Journal of the North American Reggio Emilia Alliance), 10 (2), 1–4.

Rinaldi, C. (2006) 'In dialogue with Carlina Rinaldi', in *In Dialogue with Reggio Emilia: Listening, Researching and Learning*, Routledge, Abingdon.

Rinaldi, C. (2007) Notes from address at Environments for Enquiry Conference, University of York, UK.

Seidel, S. (2002) Presentation at ReFocus One Symposium, June, Kendal, UK.

UK Study Tour (2000a) Notes from visit to the Diana municipal preschool.

UK Study Tour (2000b) 'Relationship between the school and the environment in respect of a day in the life of the school'. Seminar presentation to UK Study Group, October, Reggio Emilia.

UK Study Tour (2000c) Notes from discussion with staff at La Villetta municipal preschool.

7 Creativity

Alphabets of String[1]

rolled up

pasta knot

mummified string

interlaced

tangled

string in a maze

knotty string

line of string

ghosty string

Creativity seems to express itself through cognitive, affective and imaginative processes. These come together and support the skills for predicting and arriving at unexpected solutions.

(Malaguzzi 1998: 76)

This chapter focuses on the creativity of thought and expression that lies at the heart of the Reggio philosophy. It considers the origins of this way of working, reflects on the nature of creativity and looks at how all the different elements of the Reggio Approach come together to nurture children's creative learning experiences. The importance of the environment, the role of the adult, and the availability of creative resources in facilitating creative expression are discussed. Finally, two examples of young children's creativity, one from an infant–toddler centre and the other from a preschool, serve to illustrate the intensity and care with which children look at, and make sense of, very ordinary things.

The importance of creativity

Creativity lies at the heart of the way educators in Reggio Emilia work with young children. By nurturing young children's creative expression, educators demonstrate how they value each child as an individual with his or her own ideas and abilities and unique ways of understanding and connecting with the world. All aspects of the Reggio Approach detailed in the other chapters of this book contribute to, and are enhanced by, this focus on children's and adults' creativity.

In Reggio, creativity is regarded not as belonging to any specific area of knowledge, but rather as a way of thinking, and of searching and re-searching in an attempt to make sense of the world.

As Carlina Rinaldi says:

> By creativity I mean the ability to construct new connections between thoughts and objects that bring about innovation and change, taking known elements and creating new connections. . . . What we hope for is creative learning and creative teachers, not simply a 'creativity hour'. We should remember that there is no creativity in the child if there is no creativity in the adult: the competent and creative child exists if there is a competent and creative adult.
>
> (Rinaldi 2006: 91)

The origins of this emphasis on fostering children's creativity lie in the particular historical, cultural and political circumstances that gave rise to the beginnings of the Reggio Approach at the end of the Second World War (see Chapter 1). The parents, who were instrumental in establishing the first preschools, were adamant that they would never again bring up a generation of children who did not ask questions about what was happening to them. They were intent on giving their children the opportunity to take control of their own destinies rather than finding themselves the victims of whatever society foisted upon them (Malaguzzi 1998: 50). For very practical reasons, in their early days the preschools were heavily dependent on the resources and materials that were available free of charge in the local community. As Emilia Romagna is in a ceramics area, these free materials included clay – an ideal open-ended resource for creative expression.

Loris Malaguzzi, in his role as the pedagogical inspiration and mentor of the Reggio Approach, was a man of many talents and interests. He combined his understanding of child psychology and education with an interest in art, music, literature, science, sport and politics. His belief that all adults working with young children should share their abilities and interests led to the development of the two specialised roles of pedagogista and atelierista (see Chapter 2). All adults working in the Reggio preschools and infant–toddler centres are expected to have a keen interest in the world around them, to hold and express opinions and to enter into discussion and debate with colleagues, parents and children.

Creative expression

By valuing young children's ideas and interpretations of the world, educators in Reggio encourage children to formulate and express their own opinions and to learn to listen to, and value, the opinions of others. This two-way exchange of ideas helps a child to recognise his or her own individuality and at the same time develop an appreciation of the way in which society connects us all together. Educators recognise that children have many different ways of communicating their thoughts and ideas and have, over many years, developed their skills in recognising and responding to children's creative thinking and modes of expression.

The concept of children and adults as co-constructors of knowledge demonstrates that adults respect and value children's ideas, thoughts and perspectives on the world. It is the bringing together of these two different ways of looking at the world which builds the knowledge and understanding of both parties – adults and children (see Chapter 6). Experiences offered to young children in Reggio are rooted in the real world and not an adult's interpretation of what is suitable or convenient for young children to know and experience. For example, should an appropriate opportunity arise, young children are encouraged to think about and express their feelings about very profound and serious subjects such as birth, death and war. By encouraging creative expression, the Reggio Approach encourages individuals to find their own solutions to problems and challenges through communicating ideas, exploring thoughts and emotions, or creating objects of worth and beauty.

Creative spaces

The environments of the preschools and infant–toddler centres are aesthetically designed and beautifully presented. They are created to facilitate children's independent exploration and discovery (see Chapter 3). The atelier epitomises the concept of the preschool or infant–toddler centre as a place of creative learning, housing art materials, natural resources, reclaimed resources, clay, wire, digital technology equipment and musical instruments.

The notion of the atelier was fundamental to Loris Malaguzzi's vision of early education:

> I will not hide from you how much hope we invested in the introduction of the atelier. We knew it would be impossible to ask for anything more. Yet, if we could have done so we would have gone further still by creating a school made entirely of laboratories similar to the atelier. We would have constructed a new type of school made of spaces where the hands of children could be active for messing about. With no possibility of boredom, hands and minds would engage each other with great, liberating merriment in a way ordained by biology and evolution.
>
> (Malaguzzi 1998: 73–4)

The atelier is not just a physical space within a building, but is also a symbol representing the value and importance of creativity. Creative expression does not happen just within the atelier, but is manifest in everything that takes place indoors and outdoors within a preschool or infant–toddler centre. The open-ended equipment, including mirrors and light boxes, that can be found throughout the centres encourages creative thinking and expression.

As Carlina Rinaldi comments:

> The atelier is a metaphorical space in schools which, taken as a whole, aims to support the development of communication and the hundred languages. I believe there is a distinction to be made: the difference that I sense exists between atelier and studio workshop. It is not just a linguistic distinction, it is a difference in concept and pedagogy.
>
> (Rinaldi 2006: 176)

Time to be creative

The organisation of the day gives children all of the time they need to become immersed in the activities and experiences that interest them (see Chapter 5). The day is structured to give children as much autonomy as possible over their use of time, within a framework of carefully negotiated and agreed parameters which define each individual's roles and responsibilities.

Ideas and experiences, some of which may result in long-term projects, are often introduced as provocations. The term 'provocation' describes a stimulus or trigger for creative thought or action. This may be in the form of an object, an experience, an idea, a question or a challenge which provokes a reaction of some nature. When introducing new provocations, educators often make use of the concept of 'wait time' in order to give children time to think about their creative ideas (UK Study Tour 2005). Instead of expecting children to come up with wonderful ideas immediately, educators introduce a provocation, have a very brief discussion about it and then leave the children time to think and reflect. Several days may elapse before they revisit the provocation, by which time the children have had time to consider their ideas and formulate their questions.

Adults as creative enablers

Educators in Reggio appreciate the importance of strong, positive relationships between staff, parents and children (see Chapter 4). This creates the emotional climate in which children feel comfortable to ask questions, put forward ideas, be imaginative and try things out. Children frequently work together in small groups. This enables children to share skills, knowledge and experience with one another but also creates an environment for cognitive challenge as they share and explain ideas.

Young children's creativity is supported by creative adults who share their skills and competencies. Children are taught the skills which enable them to use tools and materials competently so they can learn to make safe choices and deal with risk and challenge. They learn the skills and techniques of drawing, painting, working with clay, or handling digital technology equipment in order to make use of these skills in expressing their creative thoughts and ideas. The atelierista has a particular role in sharing creative skills with the children but all adults are expected to play a role in supporting young children's creative thinking.

Through focused discussion and skilful questioning, children are helped to reflect on their learning and to re-examine and redefine their ideas and thoughts. From a very young age, children are encouraged to use graphic representation as a tool to capture their ideas and theories. Ideas first expressed verbally are re-presented in drawings and paintings and through 3-D models. Through explaining their drawings and models to their peers and to adults, children refine their thinking and deepen their understanding.

Documentation of young children's thinking and learning through the use of photographs, transcripts of conversations, sketches, drawings and models enables educators to share their interpretations and understanding of what young children are thinking and learning (see Chapter 8). Sharing multiple perspectives in this way emphasises the contribution which all adults – teachers, pedagogistas, atelieristas and parents – can bring to furthering the understanding of young children's cognitive processes. Interpreting documentation gives educators the information they need to plan what opportunities to offer children next in order to consolidate their learning.

Creative resources

Open-ended exploration is supported through the provision of a wide range of natural and reclaimed materials. Children are encouraged to respect and value these resources and to look upon them as 'intelligent materials' with enormous creative possibilities.

The children are provided with a wide range of opaque, translucent and transparent materials such as beads, glass nuggets, buttons, small bottles, plastic and metal discs to investigate using light boxes and the overhead projector. Glass, in the form of containers, mirrors, pendants, balls and bottles is a commonly found resource – used by children of all ages. These reclaimed resources are complemented by natural materials including driftwood, stones, shells, cones, leaves, seed pods and feathers.

From the earliest age, children investigate the properties and expressive potential of clay and wire. Clay, which is abundant in the Emilia Romagna region, is valued for its transformational properties, ideal for moving ideas from one context to another. It is used as a key medium for children to acquire manipulative skills, develop ideas over a long period of time, and create objects of beauty and value. Its malleability invites children to make and remake forms as their ideas and imagination take hold. Wire shares much of the expressive potential of clay. It can be bent, shaped, twisted and joined to create open, 'empty' images which invite closer investigation and interpretation.

Traditional art materials such as paint, pens, pencils and paper are provided for the children. For drawing, they are offered choices from a range of mark-making materials, including soft lead pencils, coloured pencils and black or coloured markers with fine or large tips. Paints and inks are provided in subtle gradations of shade and tone to encourage close observation and colour memory. Paper is offered in a range of colours, shapes, sizes and textures.

Throughout the preschools and infant–toddler centres, the space is organised to enable children to freely access the resources and materials they need. Everything is out in the open where it can be seen; children know where things are and can find, use and return them.

As Amelia Gambetti, Executive Coordinator of the Reggio Children organisation, explained:

> In Reggio we have the highest quality kinds of materials we can find, not so the children can become geniuses but so that they and we have many opportunities to discover their learning processes and their abilities to think. I believe that when you give this to children when they are so young, when you empower them in their thinking, it stays with them forever – as Malaguzzi used to say, like an extra pocket. They understand the power of their intelligence.
>
> (Gambetti 2003: 76)

REMIDA Creative Recycling Centre

Many of the resources are provided through the REMIDA Creative Recycling Centre, a project between the Municipality of Reggio Emilia and the Agency for Energy and Environmental Services (AGAC), and managed by the Friends of Reggio Children International Association.

Through the REMIDA project, reject, surplus and recycled materials from local industries are collected to provide resources for creative projects in the community.

In the REMIDA centre the recycled resources – including plastics and packaging of many kinds, fabrics, metal, electrical components, string, glass, wire, rubber, hide, yarns, papers and card – are exquisitely displayed in what has been described as 'a warehouse of wonders'. The materials are arranged to be captivating and stimulating; they are not randomly arranged, but are displayed in an ordered and beautiful way. Visitors are encouraged to explore the resources with all their senses, using magnifiers and stethoscopes to appreciate their visual and acoustic properties.

REMIDA is not only a warehouse, it is also a cultural centre that organises training sessions and workshops led by artists, designers and other creative professionals. Children often visit the centre, not to make things, but to explore and investigate the materials and choose the items they want to use creatively back in their preschool environment. Families also have the opportunity to visit the centre and use the resources.

Every year, during the month of May, special days of celebration take place when the many piazzas and elegant boulevards of the city are transformed by displays and events inspired by the concept of REMIDA. These events have included a second-hand market, interactions between the performing arts, large-scale installations made of reclaimed materials, and the construction of a 500 metre 'REchocolate cake' made from 10,000 unsold Easter eggs and stale bread. Pride of place is given to projects designed and constructed by the children and staff of the preschools, which are often placed in the windows of various shops in the city (Ferrari and Giacopini 2005).

Creativity in action

Many of the projects described in other chapters of this book – 'Theatre Curtain' (pages 78–81) (Vecchi 2002), 'Blacks and Whites' (pages 114–15) (Vecchi and Giudici 2004), and 'Stories of Air' (page 117) (Sturloni 2004) – provide vivid examples of young children's creativity. The following examples, both taken from the 'City in Waiting' project, which involved many of the preschools and infant–toddler centres, illustrate the way in which simple everyday experiences can act as powerful provocations to unleash young children's creativity. Over the course of a year, groups of children made repeated visits to three areas of the city of Reggio Emilia to explore the environment using all their senses. Back in the centres, these experiences formed the basis for discussion and reflection, giving children the opportunity to re-present their ideas, feelings and emotions and to express, in many different ways, their own perspective of the city. Many of their representations were incorporated in the annual REMIDA day celebrations, giving the inhabitants of the city the opportunity to gain an insight into young children's views of the world they inhabit.

'The park is . . .'

Children from the Bellelli infant–toddler centre explored the large park in the centre of the city (Cavallini *et al.* 2008). Educators were conscious of the need to give children time to satisfy their curiosity, to pay close attention to the way in which children explored their surroundings, and to respect children's diverse forms of creative expression.

> Our times are dominated by ideas of knowledge as linear development and strong trends for accelerating children's learning. Instead children's strategies for thinking and acting, their extraordinary sense of invention, invite us to remark just how much and in what ways creativity, play and expression and aesthetic sense together with the times and rhythms of reflection and knowledge, are capable of combining and transforming, of emotion and analysis, empathy and connection. They are a vital, a structuring part of the educational process.
>
> (Cavallini *et al.* 2008: 11)

As part of their exploration, the 18- to 24-month-old children were intrigued by the sound qualities of the different places and materials they encountered. They tapped the trees and the ground with sticks, dragged sticks through the leaves and the gravel, knocked large stones together and listened carefully to the sounds of small pebbles dropping into a metal waste bin. One of the children pushed four short sticks into a cavity between two stones, tapped them with another stick and discovered he had made a 'sound machine'. Back in the infant–toddler centre these experiences were discussed and reflected on and children were given opportunities to create more sound machines using sticks and clay and to explore the sounds which different natural materials make. Their comments and reactions were captured in words and photographs and through a audio recording of their 'sound explorations'.

You need a stick that hits other sticks, so you can hear the sound of rain.
You hit it soft and the rain falls soft . . .
You hit it hard and it's a storm!

My nose is as full as a world

Groups of children from the Balducci preschool explored the Via Farini, one of the many old streets in Reggio leading to the city centre (Balducci 2005). The children went on frequent visits to Via Farini to explore it using all their senses. They looked at colours, listened to sounds, touched walls, pavements and street signs and commented on the smells of the street. The imagination of one group of children was fired by the range of different smells they encountered.

On Via Farini there's the smell of flowers.
From the church comes the smell of the body of Christ, of fire and candle smoke.
There's the wall smell . . . the bridge smell, like the wall smell.
Then we caught the bus, if you go close you smell the tyre smell and inside
   there's the ticket smell.
I smell the cigarette smell . . . the coffee bar smell . . . the croissant smell . . .
I have smelled the smells with my nose and I found the right street.

Back in the preschool the children's interest in scents and smells was fostered through provocations and experiences which encouraged them to explore in more depth their understanding and emotional responses to smells. Children created graphic representations of different smells in drawings, paintings and clay models. They discussed ways of creating a 'smell transformer catcher machine' to capture all the different smells in Via Farini and represented them in words and drawings.

There are two tubes: one for good smells and one for bad smells. After the machine has caught the smells, it throws them out into the city, but only the good smells! The bad smells are thrown out in another city . . .

As Loris Malaguzzi so aptly put it,

Creativity? It is always difficult to notice when it is dressed in everyday clothing and has the ability to appear and disappear suddenly. Our task, regarding creativity, is to help children climb their own mountains, as high as possible. No one can do more.

(Malaguzzi 1998: 77)

Key points

1. Creativity does not belong to one specific area of knowledge or experience.
2. Nurturing young children's creative thinking and expression is dependent on the input of creative adults.
3. Children express their ideas, thoughts and emotions in many different ways, using their hundred languages of expression.
4. The beautiful, ordered environment of the preschools and infant–toddler centres supports young children's creative expression.
5. The atelier is not just a place for creative activity, but also a symbol of the importance of keeping creativity at the heart of young children's learning.
6. Children need time to think about and reflect on their ideas, and time to revisit experiences to deepen their understanding.
7. Creativity is sparked by provocations – objects, experiences, ideas, questions or challenges which provoke a reaction.
8. Working together in groups enables children to share skills and experience and to enjoy the cognitive challenge of explaining and justifying their ideas and opinions.
9. Open-ended natural and reclaimed resources provide children with opportunities to re-present their creative ideas.
10. REMIDA, the creative recycling centre, is an important symbol of the value and potential of simple everyday objects.

Reflections on the Reggio Approach

1. Creativity as a way of thinking:
   - How do you demonstrate that children's creative thinking is valued across all areas of learning?
   - Do you make good use of questions, conversations and discussions with children to reflect on their ideas?
   - How do you share children's creative thoughts and ideas with other children, colleagues and parents?
2. Creative spaces:
   - Does your environment contain interesting provocations to stimulate creative thinking?
   - Do children of all ages have access to mirrors and light boxes?
   - Are you making the best use of creative opportunities available out of doors?

3. Time to be creative:
   - Do children have time during the day to become immersed in experiences which fascinate them?
   - How often can children return to an experience to deepen and extend their understanding?
   - Could you make use of the idea of 'wait time' when introducing a new provocation?
4. The role of the adult:
   - How do you share your own creativity with the children?
   - How attentive are you to the different forms of creative expression which children of different ages use?
   - Are you an enthusiastic role model for curiosity and possibility thinking?
5. Creative resources:
   - Do children have access to a wide range of interesting reclaimed and natural resources?
   - Are resources attractively presented and accessible?
   - How cluttered is your environment – do you need all that stuff?

Note

1. *'Children, Art, Artists: The Expressive Language of Children: The Artistic Language of Alberto Burri'* © Municipality of Reggio Emilia, Infant–Toddler Centres and Preschools, published by Reggio Children, Reggio Emilia, 2001, p. 43.

References

Balducci preschool (2005) *My Nose is as Full as the World*, Reggio Children, Reggio Emilia.

Cavallini, I., Filippini, T., Trancossi, L. and Vecchi, V. (eds) (2008) *The Park is . . .*, Reggio Children, Reggio Emilia.

Ferrari, A. and Giacopini, E. (eds) (2005) *REMIDA Day*, Reggio Children, Reggio Emilia.

Gambetti, A. (2003) 'Teachers living in collaboration', in Cadwell, L. B. *Bringing Learning to Life. The Reggio Approach to Early Childhood Education*, Teachers College Press, Columbia University, New York and London, pp. 67–100.

Malaguzzi, L. (1998) 'History, ideas and basic philosophy', in Edwards, C., Gandini, L. and Forman, G. (eds) *The Hundred Languages of Children: The Reggio Emilia Approach – Advanced Reflections* (2nd edn), Albex, Stamford, CT, pp. 49–97.

Rinaldi, C. (2006) *In Dialogue with Reggio Emilia*, Routledge, London, pp. 91, 176.

Sturloni, S. (2004) 'Stories of air'. Presentation at Science Among Research, Poetry and Beauty seminar. Crossing Boundaries International Conference, February, Reggio Emilia.

UK Study Tour (2005) Notes from a visit to Paolo Freire preschool.

Vecchi, V. (ed.) (2002) *Theatre Curtain*, Reggio Children.

Vecchi, V. and Giudici, C. (2004) 'Blacks and Whites', in *Children, Art, Artists. The Expressive Languages of Children: The Artistic Language of Alberto Burri*, Reggio Children, Reggio Emilia, pp. 20–5.

8 Documentation

I've never seen a baby being born. I don't know who decides about being born: the mother or the babies. I don't know, I don't remember anything.[1]

Documentation is not a technique, it is a way of guaranteeing that we are always reflective and valuing the other point of view. Documentation demonstrates the knowledge of the children, our path of knowledge about a child and about ourselves. Documentation is a dialogue of the children's learning and our own development and knowledge.

(Rinaldi 2002)

This chapter looks at the many different uses of documentation, focusing on its principal purpose – planning for the next stages in children's learning on a daily basis. Different ways of gathering information are discussed, as well as the type of evidence to look for and record, both with babies and with older children. Two examples of the use of documentation are given, one from a project involving babies and toddlers and the other with 5- and 6-year-old children. Finally, the chapter looks at documentation as a means of communicating the importance of early childhood to the wider world.

Documentation – observation and interpretation

Documentation underpins the whole approach to understanding young children's learning in the preschools and infant–toddler centres of Reggio Emilia. It is seen as a way of listening to, respecting and supporting individuals in their search to make meaning of the world (Rinaldi 1998: 113). It requires sensitivity to different forms of expression and behaviour, observing with all the senses, and sharing and interpreting these observations with others (Rinaldi 1999a: 9; 2001: 78).

Documentation shows how children acquire knowledge, how they organise and process knowledge, and how they carry out research. Documentation also evidences how teachers listen to children, how they increase their knowledge with, and about, children, and how they value children and their ways of learning (International Students and Professors Study Group 2006).

Documentation involves both observation and interpretation – educators in Reggio speak of a web of reciprocal interpretation or a spiral of documentation, see Figure 8.1 (Rinaldi 2000).

Observation, in this context, is more than looking, or seeing; it also involves listening and emotional awareness. It is important to recognise that observation is not an objective process – in the act of choosing what to observe and record, the observer selects what is meaningful to them (Rinaldi 2000).

The documentation process is seen as a way of listening to the young child, valuing him as a holder and builder of theories, questions and ideas. Teachers take time for listening, recognising children as carriers of culture and co-protagonists in the acquisition of knowledge. Documentation is not just a record of the processes of learning; the mutual exchange of ideas and theories between the children and their teachers

Figure 8.1 The spiral of documentation

(Rinaldi 2000)

shows documentation as a form of visible listening to children (International Students and Professors Study Group 2006).

One of the early examples of documentation which has become well known across the world is the set of photographs and written observations showing the sequence of events when a year-old toddler, Laura, encounters the ticking of a watch for the first time. This documentation was originally included in a diary which was used by educators to record significant milestones in Laura's learning and development, to analyse and reflect upon them, and to share their thoughts and plans with parents.

> The photographs not only capture precious moments in the life of one young child but also illustrate many aspects of the educational process in Reggio Emilia, including the teachers' strong belief in and valuing of the rich resourceful and competent child, the crucial importance of pedagogical documentation and the relationship and reciprocity between adults and children in the process of learning and making connections.
>
> (Millikan 2009: 85)

The wealth of documentation enables teachers to read and interpret, re-visit, assess and self-assess continually. Documentation is seen as a continuity tool so that

> the teacher, being able to reflect on how the learning is proceeding . . . can base her teaching not on what she wants to teach, but on what the child wants to learn. . . . in this way she learns how to teach, and teacher and children together search for the best way to proceed.
>
> (Rinaldi 2006: 78)

Educators in Reggio have refined and developed their skills of observation and interpretation over many years but are quick to point out that interpreting documentation is not easy, especially with babies – it is a challenge to interpret their languages. 'We are in distress – they know how to express themselves, we don't know how to interpret' (Giacopini 2004).

Using documentation to support individual and group learning

Documenting the learning processes of children involves capturing evidence of skills, dispositions and feelings; conversations and discussions; interactions and relationships; gesture, stance and posture. Using this evidence, observations made and interpreted by an individual educator are shared and reinterpreted, on a daily basis, with colleagues. At the same time, plans are made regarding the materials, resources and opportunities which will be presented to the children the following day. New possibilities for observation are discussed and the next cycle of the observation/interpretation process begins (UK Study Tour 2000a).

The teachers, atelierista and pedagogista meet weekly to review the documentation and to share observations and interpretations. The atelierista helps to interpret the graphic languages used by children and to draw attention to other forms of expression which may have been used. The role of the pedagogista is to identify the concepts that underlie the children's work, and reflect on the meanings and interpretations which have been made (Filippini 2005: 68). The information gained is used to understand more about the learning of the individuals within a group, and of the group itself. From this, the educators are able to forecast, hypothesise and plan a strategy for the following week.

The uses of documentation

For **teachers**, documentation provides the evidence of how children's learning develops. It is an important part of continuing professional development as it offers the teacher a unique opportunity to reflect – to re-listen, re-see and re-visit, either individually or with others, the events and processes in which she played a part.

For **children**, documentation gives an opportunity for reflection and self-assessment. By looking at photographs or video recordings, or listening to audio recordings of discussions they have taken part in, children can revisit previous experiences and remember their ideas and theories. They can see themselves interacting with others in group situations and, over time, are able to observe how their skills and competencies have developed. The care with which children's pictures, drawings and words are displayed gives powerful messages about the value that is placed on what they say and do (Katz 1998: 38).

For **parents**, documentation helps them to know what their child does and how they learn. It gives them an insight into the daily life of their children while they are at an infant–toddler centre or preschool and provides a starting point for communication with their children and with teachers. The presence of documentation panels lining the walls of the centres fosters a wider interest in the learning of all children (Malaguzzi 1998: 70).

For the **wider community**, documentation offers the opportunity to demonstrate the competence of children and the ongoing research into understanding learning processes. It reinforces the concept of citizenship and is a way of celebrating the investment in early childhood services made by the whole community. The presence of the Loris Malaguzzi International Centre in the city of Reggio Emilia makes learning visible to its citizens.

The tools of documentation

The way in which documentary evidence is collected depends on the context of the learning situation. Photographs, videos, written notes, drawings, audio recordings, and annotated charts are all used, as well as two-dimensional (2-D) and 3-D examples of children's work – in progress as well as finished. Teachers then spend time during the working day organising and transcribing this information to make it available for sharing with their colleagues.

Educators in Reggio are skilled in the arts of photography and videography: capturing the thinking and learning processes of children and adults using digital images and video. The children also record their own learning and experiences using digital photography, often demonstrating high levels of technical competence.

Documentation involves not only visual images, but also capturing the context of these images by recording the words which children use to express their questions and ideas. Children's theories and conversations are recorded using audio recorders and as written transcripts. Notes and sketches made by the educators during discussions with the children are also used as a record of what the children say and do.

At the different stages of the development of long-term projects, the children will have represented their ideas, theories and opinions through a variety of media – conversation, drawings, paintings, models, music and movement. These representations add to the portfolio of evidence as part of the documentation process.

Documentation with babies and toddlers

Documentation in the infant–toddler centres begins with building an understanding of how parents view their children. In addition to information about sleeping patterns and feeding routines, the teachers 'gather the words that the parents use to give shape to their children'. They use this information, provided by parents at the initial visit, to create verbal portraits of the children (UK Study Tour 2000b).

Documentation is used to look closely into how young children enter into relationships with themselves, each other and their environment, through verbal exchanges, mimicry, looks, expression, gestures and action. Situations are created where small groups of children can play together and materials that will stimulate curiosity, creativity, communication and activity are provided. Stones, shells, wood, pine cones and translucent materials are used in combination with natural light, torches and the overhead projector. They investigate these objects by looking, touching, lifting, turning, smelling and shaking, increasing their familiarity with the properties of materials – hard and soft, rough and smooth, sharp and rounded, shiny and dull, heavy and light.

Individual and group learning is recorded through photographs, video and written observations, as well as the children's creations, compositions and early words (Giudici *et al.* 2001a: 10; 2001b: 34).

'Blacks and Whites': an example of documentation with babies and toddlers

'Blacks and Whites' was part of a wider research project looking at the relationships between children, art and artists. The focus for the project was the question: 'What elements can establish a relationship between children from eight months to two years old and a mature and famous artist like Alberto Burri?' (Vecchi and Giudici 2004: 20).

Two infant–toddler centres worked with their Infants group (6–10 months) and Toddlers 2 group (18–24 months) to investigate blacks and whites.

During the course of 'Blacks and Whites' one infant–toddler centre worked with the colour black and the other with white, using different types of plastic, paper and fabric. Traditionally, black and white are symbolic, with black rarely associated with the world of young children. The research found that children approached black and white with equal curiosity, thought both colours beautiful, and were able to recognise a range of shades (Vecchi and Giudici 2004: 17).

The documentation of the project consisted of:

■ visual images of the children interacting with the materials and with each other;
■ detailed written observations of their actions;
■ the compositions and arrangements of materials created by the children;
■ transcripts of the words used by the children.

'There are black blacks, and there are more coloured blacks' (C. 32 months). 'They're whites; they're not all the same' (E. 24 months).

For the Infants group, carpets were created of carefully chosen black and white materials. The documentation showed the children using their bodies to explore relationships with these materials and the boundaries and thresholds of the carpets. They used a multi-sensory approach to their investigations – feeling, hearing, smelling, tasting, as well as looking – over long periods of time.

For the research with Toddlers 2, the investigations centred on a range of black or white materials which the children had helped to compile. Individually, they used different strategies to explore the materials but also paid a great deal of attention to the gestures and actions of the other children. The documentation clearly demonstrated the early stages of group learning and understanding.

For teachers, the documentation provided a way of recording the detail of children's actions, gestures and expressions to inform their understanding of the depth and quality of the children's research.

For children, the documentation created a memory bank of their competency in understanding, transforming and composing the materials.

The project prompted the development of slide presentations for the families of the children of the infant–toddler centres and preschools. It also generated material for professional development opportunities for educators, artists and museum staff in Italy and abroad.

Documentation with preschool children

With preschool children, the images and transcripts collected in the process of documentation portray individuals and groups, communication and exchange, discussion and debate, ideas and theories, and when appropriate, the final product. They convey important information about the skills of individual children and the way in which they use self-assessment to structure their own learning. They also provide the opportunity to observe social interactions between children and use these to build strategies for cooperation, collaboration and peer learning (Vecchi 2001: 158).

The detail with which learning is documented on a daily basis is evident from the following extract describing a small group of preschool children using clay (UK Study Tour 2000a). The documentation which the teacher compiled during one morning session in the preschool included:

- a description of the focus for the observation – the relationship between hands and clay;
- a record of the context – who was there, how the group was formed and arranged, what tools and materials they were using and how long they were there;
- sketches of the process of each individual child's clay work using a numbered sequence of observations on a group recording sheet, including a record of the mood of each child;
- a description of both individual and group progress;
- a description of teacher intervention showing when and how intervention had occurred;
- audio recordings of what the children had said;
- the children's working drawings and designs;
- the final representations in clay.

The verbal descriptions and photographic representations were then shared with other adults for discussion to gather different perspectives on the learning process that had taken place. The visual images, combined with the record of the spoken and written word, elegantly demonstrated the complexity of the children's cognitive and social development.

'Stories of Air': an example of documentation with preschool children

The stimulus for this project came from children's awareness of the smell of flowers in the preschool garden, prompting the question: 'What is scent and how can you describe it?'

The documentation of 'Stories of Air' included:

- recordings of the words children had used to describe their theories about what smells were, where they came from and how we respond to them: 'Smells come from the earth – they go up the stalk, round to the centre of the flower and then down again. A little bit comes off and goes up your nose'; 'If you see what the smell is, your nose will recognise it';
- the creation of an olfactory map of the school, inside and out, with photographs and drawings linking places with the memories and reactions they invoked;
- close observational drawing of flowers, plants and leaves linked to theories about how and where scent was created;
- visualising smells through drawings and *mandalas* made from natural materials, using the colour, texture, pattern, shape and form to express the nature of a scent and make the invisible visible;
- recordings of the process of designing a 'smell and guess' box to increase olfactory awareness;
- tracking, in words and pictures, the discussions and investigations involved in an experiment to extract the scent from rose petals;
- the creation by the children of an instruction booklet designed to help another group of children to carry out the investigation into rose perfume.

During the course of the project, documentation was used to help teachers track children's understanding of the nature of scents and smells, and for them to share these experiences and perspectives with colleagues. Through this process, teachers extended their own understanding of how the children had approached learning, solved problems and constructed meanings.

Documentation helped the children to retain, and remember, the thread running through their learning, and to investigate different ways of communicating their ideas to others.

For parents and the community, documentation connected the daily life of the preschool to the wider world as well as giving an insight into the children's learning and understanding of the world (Sturloni 2004).

Documentation for communication

Within the infant–toddler centres and preschools, documentation is displayed on panels on the walls throughout the school. The documentation panels are created in the Centre for Documentation and Research, based at the Loris Malaguzzi International Centre, under the supervision of a member of the pedagogical team. These visually appealing and intellectually challenging displays are a tool for communication between the school and the family and the outside world. They illustrate the experiences, long-term projects and various activities of the children and tell the observer much about the life and values of the school.

The complete information is archived and drawn upon periodically as a resource for ongoing professional development, but some examples of the documentation of projects are retained in the schools for long periods of time – traces of the past which create a collective memory of the life and activity of the school (Spaggiari 2004).

The Hundred Languages of Children exhibition and the newer exhibitions *The Wonder of Learning* and *Atelier Ray of Light,* along with the many publications produced by the Reggio Children organisation, draw upon this wealth of action research-based evidence of children's imagination, creativity and learning processes. For many people, their first experience of the work of the infant–toddler centres and pre-schools of Reggio Emilia is *The Hundred Languages of Children* exhibition. Created by Loris Malaguzzi in the early 1980s under the original title *The Eye, if it Leaps Over the Wall,* it illustrates his image of childhood and demonstrates the value of research. Several versions of the exhibition have travelled the world under the management of Reggio Children.

In the words of Loris Malaguzzi: 'It is an exhibition which should testify to the pleasure and the fatigue of learning, the joy of discovery, of formulating hypotheses and theories; it should testify to the struggle against boredom . . .' (Malaguzzi 2004).

The new exhibition *The Wonder of Learning*, is a stunning and thought-provoking example of children's enquiry, creativity, intelligence and resourcefulness, telling the story of children, teachers and education today. It also records the way in which the documentation of children's learning in Reggio has developed since 1981.

Documentation sits at the heart of the Reggio Approach. In the words of Carlina Rinaldi:

> Just like an unfinished piece of music, the documents produced by the children and teachers cry out to be interpreted, reinterpreted and modified. They are stories that never end, because their completion lies in the unfinished dialogue between their author, interpreter and us as we set about listening, reinterpreting and reliving a learning experience or experience of life.
>
> (Rinaldi 1999b)

Key points

1. Documentation underpins the whole approach to understanding young children's learning in the preschools and infant–toddler centres.
2. Documentation involves both observation and interpretation, and values multiple perspectives and viewpoints.
3. Evidence of skills, dispositions, interactions and relationships can be captured through the process of documentation.
4. The principal purpose of documentation is to gather evidence of children's learning on a daily basis and to use this information to plan for the next stages of learning.
5. Written information – comments and conversations – provides the context for the visual images.
6. Gathering documentary evidence requires planning and skill as well as time for transcription and organisation of information.
7. Documentation helps children to reflect on their ideas and helps to keep the thread of learning intact from day to day.
8. Documentation helps parents to understand more about the abilities and competence of their children and keeps them connected with the life of the school.
9. The availability of documentation creates a rich resource for continuing professional development.

10. The care and attention given to the collection and display of children's ideas and research conveys very powerful messages about the value and status of early childhood.

Reflections on the Reggio Approach

1. Tools of documentation:
   - What skills, resources and equipment do you already have which could support the documentation process?
   - How could you gain any skills or technical expertise which would be useful?
   - In what ways can you help children be actively involved in the documentation process?
2. Knowing what to document:
   - How do the observation techniques and recording systems you currently use need to be revised in order to focus more closely on the process of learning rather than the product?
   - How closely do you pay attention to, and record, the detail of children's interactions, particularly those of very young children?
   - Do you capture the exact words the children use to describe their ideas and thoughts?
3. Using documentation to plan children's learning:
   - How can you use documentation, gathered and reviewed on a daily basis, to replace some of your existing planning and recording systems?
   - What restructuring of the day is needed to create time for this process to happen?
4. Using documentation with children and parents:
   - Do children use documentation to revisit their ideas and develop their understanding?
   - Could you make better use of documentation – contextualised displays, booklets detailing projects – to help parents feel connected with their children's learning?
5. Wider uses of documentation:
   - How could documentation be used as a part of a programme of continuous professional development?
   - Is there a value in retaining and displaying evidence of past projects as part of the history of the institution?
   - Are there opportunities to use documentation to raise the status of early childhood within the local community?

Note

1. *The Hundred Languages of Children: Catalogue of the Exhibition* © Municipality of Reggio Emilia – Infant–Toddler Centres and Preschools, published by Reggio Children, Reggio Emilia, 1996, p. 204.

References

Filippini, T. (2005) 'The atelier and the role of the pedagogical co-ordinator', in Gandini, L., Cadwell, L. and Schwall, C. (eds) *In the Spirit of the Studio*, Teachers College Press, Columbia University, New York and London, p. 68.

Giacopini, E. (2004) 'The right to environment. Children, spaces, relations. Pedagogy and architecture'. Seminar at Crossing Boundaries International Conference, February, Reggio Emilia.

Giudici, C., Rinaldi, C. and Krechevsky, M. (2001a) 'Contagious experiments', in *Making Learning Visible: Children as Individual and Group Learners*, Reggio Children, pp. 10–15.

Giudici, C., Rinaldi, C. and Krechevsky, M. (2001b) 'The right hand', in *Making Learning Visible: Children as Individual and Group Learners*, Reggio Children, Reggio Emilia, pp. 34–7.

International Students and Professors Study Group (2006) Notes from presentation, 'Observation, interpretation and documentation'.

Katz, L. G. (1998) 'What can we learn from Reggio Emilia?', in Edwards, C., Gandini, L. and Forman, G. (eds) *The Hundred Languages of Children: The Reggio Emilia Approach – Advanced Reflections* (2nd edn), Albex, Stamford, CT, pp. 27–45.

Malaguzzi, L. (1998) 'History, ideas and basic philosophy', in Edwards, C., Gandini, L. and Forman, G. (eds) *The Hundred Languages of Children: The Reggio Emilia Approach – Advanced Reflections* (2nd edn), Albex, Stamford, CT, pp. 49–97.

Malaguzzi, L. (2004) 'Speech in Bologna' for the opening of the *Hundred Languages of Children* exhibition in 1990, quoted in literature to accompany the Crossing Boundaries International Conference, Reggio Children, Reggio Emilia.

Millikan, J. (2009) 'Laura's diary, an Australian perspective', in Edwards, C. P. and Rinaldi, C. (eds) *The Diary of Laura – Perspectives on a Reggio Emilia Diary*, Redleaf Press, St Paul, MN, p. 85.

Rinaldi, C. (1998) 'Projected curriculum constructed through documentation – *progettazione*', in Edwards, C., Gandini, L. and Forman, G. (eds) *The Hundred Languages of Children: The Reggio Emilia Approach – Advanced Reflections* (2nd edn), Albex, Stamford, CT, pp. 113–25.

Rinaldi, C. (1999a) 'L'Ascolto Visible' (Visible listening), *rechild*, 3, 7, Reggio Children, Reggio Emilia.

Rinaldi, C. (1999b) 'The thought that sustains educational action', *rechild*, 2, 9, Reggio Children.

Rinaldi, C. (2000) 'Visible listening'. Presentation to UK Study Group, October.

Rinaldi, C. (2001) 'Documentation and assessment: what is the relationship?', in Giudici, C., Rinaldi, C. and Krechevsky, M. (eds) *Making Learning Visible: Children as Individual and Group Learners*, Reggio Children, Reggio Emilia, pp. 78–89.

Rinaldi, C. (2002) 'Teachers as researchers'. Presentation at ReFocus One Symposium, June, Kendal, UK.

Rinaldi, C. (2006) 'Documentation and research', in *In Dialogue with Reggio Emilia: Listening, Researching and Learning*, Routledge, Abingdon.

Spaggiari, A. (2004) Opening address at Crossing Boundaries International Conference, February, Reggio Emilia.

Sturloni, S. (2004) 'Stories of air'. Presentation at Science Among Research, Poetry and Beauty seminar. Crossing Boundaries International Conference, February, Reggio Emilia.

UK Study Tour (2000a) Notes from visit to the Diana municipal preschool, October.

UK Study Tour (2000b) Notes from visit to Bellelli infant–toddler centre, October.

Vecchi, V. (2001) 'The curiosity to understand', in *Making Learning Visible: Children as Individual and Group Learners*, Reggio Children, Reggio Emilia, pp. 158–212.

Vecchi, V. and Giudici, C. (2004) 'Blacks and Whites', in *Children, Art, Artists: The Expressive Languages of Children: The Artistic Language of Alberto Burri*, Reggio Children, Reggio Emilia.

9 The future

Valentina - It's a lucky bridge made of lots of May bugs flying close to each other. They make a line, a long line of May bugs.[1]

As educators it is our duty to know more about the planet of children. We know too little about how children learn and about how their ideas and opinions are formed. We need to search, and document – listening to and observing the signs, making connections and meanings understandable.

(Spaggiari 2004)

This chapter looks at recent developments in Reggio Emilia and the UK and finishes by summarising the key messages from the work of the pre-schools and infant–toddler centres which may help to guide our future thinking about early childhood and beyond.

In Reggio Emilia

The Reggio Children organisation is involved in an increasing number of projects and professional development initiatives with colleagues throughout the world. In 2004, the Crossing Boundaries International Conference, held in Reggio, brought together over 1,000 representatives from 54 different countries. During the conference, delegates were encouraged to cross geographical boundaries between countries and languages, philosophical boundaries between cultures and religious beliefs, as well as the boundaries between art, science, music, literature, philosophy and architecture, and to be open to the opportunities which then presented themselves. Contributors to the conference included educators from Reggio and educationalists, philosophers, politicians, administrators, designers, artists, engineers and scientists from Italy and the rest of the world, reflecting the diverse, multidisciplinary interest which exists in the achievements and ideals of the Reggio experience (Banfi 2004: 136).

Reggio Children has continued to host biennial Winter and Summer Institutes for international visitors. The April 2014 international study group hosted 400 participants from around the world interested in the work of the infant–toddler centres and preschools.

Reggio Children provides information via its website (www. reggiochildren.it) through a downloadable periodical, *rechild*, and the *rechild news* newsletter, and also through the Friends of Reggio Children International Association. Since 2006, international study tours have been held in the Loris Malaguzzi Centre, where programmes have often been arranged to suit particular interest groups such as professors, students, artists and atelieristas. An internship programme for educators from around the world has recently been set up, offering direct experience of working in one of the preschools or infant–toddler centres. Applicants for the programme must be students or teachers aged 30 to 40 years with a good working knowledge of spoken and written Italian.

Reggio networks of various types exist in many different parts of the world. Since 1993 there has been a Reggio Emilia Institute in Stockholm, out of which a Nordic Network developed, and in the USA the North American Reggio Emilia Alliance (NAREA) coordinates professional development initiatives and produces a quarterly journal, *Innovations*. In the southern hemisphere, the Reggio Emilia Australia Information Exchange (REAIE) links together early years educators in Australia and New Zealand and publishes a quarterly journal. The UK reference point for Reggio Children is the Sightlines Initiative based in Newcastle.

All of these different national and international initiatives reflect the outward-looking, participatory attitude of the educators in Reggio, their willingness to share research findings, and their enthusiasm to learn from the experiences of others. In 2006, the ongoing 'Tile Project' was launched where those committed to supporting and promoting the work of the educators in Reggio Emilia can have their involvement made visible through named tiles in the Malaguzzi Centre.

In the words of the Mayor of Reggio Emilia, Antonella Spaggiari, 'Reggio Emilia is part of a world-wide collaboration, accepting change as the only way forward' (Spaggiari 2004).

Jerome Bruner sees the success of the Reggio experience as arising from the fact that it is 'Small scale, high quality, under local control but with a universal set of values, thinking about the future' (Bruner 2004).

In the UK

Many people have been inspired by the work of the preschools and infant–toddler centres of Reggio Emilia, and have used this experience in different ways, to reflect on and examine their own practice. In some areas of the country, collaborative projects involving artists and early years educators have been established, and training programmes for artists wishing to work in early years settings have been organised and accredited. New ways of working have been introduced in individual settings, in groups of settings, and across local authorities, inspired by the work of Reggio, and professional development and support groups have been established. Documentation is increasingly used as a means to make young children's learning more visible to parents, colleagues and the wider public, and experience and expertise in using documentation to guide children's learning is increasing. Architects and designers involved in creating environments for young children are drawing on the design principles and research of the Domus Academy and Reggio Children.

An increasing number of early years practitioners are demonstrating how the principles underlying early years education in Reggio can fit comfortably within early years structures in the UK. The principles underlying the EYFS, introduced in England in September 2008 (Department for Children, Schools and Families 2008), have much in common with the principles of the Reggio Approach. The early years curricula of Scotland (Scottish Executive 2007) and Northern Ireland (CCEA 2006) and the Foundation Phase in Wales (Department for Children, Education, Lifelong Learning and Skills – Welsh Assembly Government 2008) resonate with the core values found in Reggio.

The approaches set out in all the UK curriculum guidance documents reinforce the importance of nurturing young children's creativity and critical thinking through first-hand experiences which build on what children already know. They advocate listening to children, observing closely to determine individual children's interests and ideas and using observational assessment to scaffold future learning. Adults are encouraged to view themselves as facilitators of children's self-initiated learning, promoting choice and independence, negotiation and collaboration, problem-solving and risk-taking.

More and more early years educators have become aware of the work of the preschools and infant–toddler centres of Reggio Emilia, through exhibitions, publications, videos and conferences. Focussed learning groups, convened by the Sightlines Initiative, exist in several parts of the UK. Sightlines also organises conferences and training events in the UK which involve presentations by educators, pedagogistas and atelieristas from Reggio Emilia. It is hoped that Reggio's most recent exhibit 'The Wonder of Learning' will be hosted in the UK in the near future.

Inspiration from Reggio Emilia

Many early years settings in the UK have taken their inspiration from their experiences in Reggio Emilia. Those who have been successful are committed to the principles of the EYFS, while drawing their inspiration from the Reggio Approach (Pace 2014).

Crucial to the success of these early years settings will be a clear understanding of the importance of learning from, but not attempting to copy, Reggio (Moss 1999; Rinaldi and Moss 2004: 3).

In summary, there seems to us to be several important lessons that we can learn from the educational experience of Reggio Emilia. Educators in Reggio speak passionately about their:

- respect for children and for childhood;
- understanding of the fundamental importance of a shared vision and values;
- appreciation of the importance of a collegiate approach which values cooperation and teamwork;
- understanding of the cultural, social, political and historical influences which have shaped their philosophy and pedagogy;
- belief that early childhood institutions are places where culture is created and values are lived on a daily basis;
- understanding that parents are entitled to help shape the future educational experience of their children;
- attention to the detail of organisation, and awareness that organisation is the key to creative and expressive freedom;
- commitment to a reflective approach that welcomes uncertainty and is comfortable with the notion of the provisional nature of knowledge;
- enthusiasm for input from a wide range of different disciplines and sources of expertise;
- willingness to recognise and respect 'difference' rather than trying to standardise it;
- use of the language of emotion alongside the language of education;
- appreciation of the continuum of time, and belief in a future full of hope and optimism.

These same principles and commitments would apply to any education professionals who are keen to investigate the possibilities of taking the Reggio Approach as an inspiration for working with older children. In Italy there is a very different national education system for children over 6 years of age and teaching and learning are very formal. In Reggio there are several initiatives taking place to explore how the curriculum for children over 6 years of age in primary schools can be approached in new ways. Within the Loris Malaguzzi Centre there is the first provision for primary-aged children alongside a preschool. The teachers are constantly modifying the way they work together across the age range. Recently, atelieristas have begun to work alongside primary teachers in several schools, which is a very new and exciting development in the schools, and a great challenge for the staff involved (Reding 2013).

While there are opportunities to see, and be inspired by, the benefits of much that the Reggio Approach to education offers in the early years, it would need a change in the thinking of government in England for teachers to feel empowered to take on the challenges which such an approach brings. As Loris Malaguzzi warned:

> School is not at all like billiards. When you play billiards you push the ball with a certain force and it hits the table and bounces off: there's a definite way the ball will go, depending on force and direction. Children are not at all like this, predictable. But sometimes schools function as if they were: these are schools with no joy.
>
> (Malaguzzi 1993)

We hope these observations, along with the 'Reflections on the Reggio Approach' at the end of each chapter, will provide starting points for reflection and discussion. Out of this may come a new understanding of what is important in early childhood, in some instances, a 'remembering' of the ideals, values and practices in which good early years education in the UK is firmly rooted (Drummond 2004).

The final words of this book come, appropriately, from Carlina Rinaldi from whom we have learned so much. 'Let us have the Utopia, which others expressed in the past, built on shared desire, hope, trust and negotiation. Let us dream together, find the passion, the curiosity and the motivation that the children can offer us' (Rinaldi 2007).

Note

1. *The Hundred Languages of Children: Catalogue of the Exhibition* © Municipality of Reggio Emilia – Infant–Toddler Centres and Preschools, published by Reggio Children, Reggio Emilia, 1996, p. 166.

References

Banfi, E. (2004) 'Sponsoring the future', in Vecchi, V. and Giudici, C. (eds) *Children, Art, Artists: The Expressive Languages of Children: The Artistic Language of Alberto Burri*, Reggio Children, Reggio Emilia, p. 136.

Bruner, J. (2004) Video address at opening session of Crossing Boundaries International Conference, February, Reggio Emilia.

CCEA (2006) *Understanding the Foundation Stage*. CCEA (Council for Curriculum, Examinations and Assessment).

Department for Children, Education, Lifelong Learning and Skills – Welsh Assembly Government (2008) *Framework for Children's Learning for 3 to 7-Year-Olds in Wales*. Available online at http://wales.gov.uk/topics/educationandskills/earlyyearshome/foundation_phase/foundationphasepractitioners/frameworkchildlearning/?lang=en (last accessed September 2014).

Department for Children, Schools and Families (2008) *The Early Years Foundation Stage: Setting the Standards for Learning, Development and Care for Children from Birth to Five*. Department for Children, Schools and Families. Available online at http://nsonline.org.uk/node/157774?uc=force_uj (last accessed September 2014).

Drummond, M. J. (2004) Address at the opening of *The Hundred Languages of Children* exhibition, June.

Malaguzzi, L. (1993) *Your Image of the Child: Where Teaching Begins*. Available online on the Reggio Alliance website www.reggioalliance.org/downloads/malaguzzi%3Accie%3A1994.pdf (last accessed September 2014).

Moss, P. (1999) 'Difference, dissensus and debate: some possibilities of learning from Reggio', *Modern Barndom OM*, Reggio Emilia Institute, Stockholm.

Pace, M. (2014) *The Joy of Learning*. Available online on the Reflections Nursery website www.reflectionsnurseries.co.uk/#/the-joy-of-learning/4575306361 (last accessed September 2014).

Reding, C. (2013) *Experiences from the Winter Institute, Reggio Emilia*. Available online on the Sightlines Initiative website www.sightlines-initiative.com/index.php?option=com_content&view=article&id=132:resource-library&catid=4:learning&Itemid=29 (last accessed September 2014).

Rinaldi, C. (2007) Notes from address at Environments for Enquiry conference, University of York, UK.

Rinaldi, C. and Moss, P. (2004) 'What is Reggio?', *Children in Europe*, 6, 2–3.

Scottish Executive (2007) *A Curriculum for Excellence – Building the Curriculum 2: Active Learning in the Early Years*. Scottish Executive. Available online at www.educationscotland.gov.uk/thecurriculum/howdoyoubuildyourcurriculum/curriculumplanning/whatisbuildingyourcurriculum/btc/btc2.asp (last accessed September 2014).

Spaggiari, S. (2004) Address at Crossing Boundaries International Conference, February, Reggio Emilia. Available online at www.nicurriculum.org.uk/docs/foundation_stage/UF_web.pdf (last accessed September 2014).

Websites

NAREA	www.reggioalliance.org
REAIE	www.reaie.org.au
Reggio Children	www.reggiochildren.it
Sightlines Initiative	www.sightlines-initiative.com

Appendix

A brief résumé of several of the publications referred to in the main text:

Advisories, Strozzi, P. and Vecchi, V. (eds) (2002), Reggio Children.
5- and 6-year-old children from the Diana School tell incoming 3-year-olds about their new preschool. This publication gives a wonderful insight into the Reggio experience as seen through the eyes of the children.

Art and Creativity in Reggio Emilia, Vecchi, V. (2010), Routledge.
This book explores the contribution of art and creativity in early education, and examines the role of the atelier and atelierista in the preschools of Reggio Emilia.

Bikes. . .Lots!, Ceppi, G. *et al.* (2014), Reggio Children.
An educational, ecological project dedicated to the topic of the bicycle which involved children and students from the infant–toddler centres through to the high schools, leading to the permanent installation in the pedestrian tunnel of the railway station of Reggio Emilia. The book presents an unusual collection of unpredictable, surprising and ironic bicycles.

Brick by Brick: The History of the 'XXV Aprile' People's Nursery School of Villa Cella (English edition), Barazzoni, R. (2000), Reggio Children.
A description of the early days of the first preschool, started on Liberation Day in 1945, through to the present day. A description of the historical, political and social influences that have helped to shape the Reggio experience.

Children, Art, Artists. The Expressive Languages of Children: The Artistic Language of Alberto Burri, Vecchi, V. and Giudici, C. (eds) (2004), Reggio Children.
A beautifully illustrated publication describing a series of projects involving children from infant–toddler through to middle-school age (8–9 years). Contains detailed descriptions of the children's interactions with recycled and natural materials as well as several essays examining the relationship between the atelier and the pedagogy in the Reggio Approach.

Children, Spaces, Relations: Metaproject for an Environment for Young Children, Ceppi, G. and Zini, M. (eds) (1998), Reggio Children.
The result of a research project looking at the relationship between pedagogy and architecture – how the physical environment can be a partner in the learning process. Contains contributions from architects, engineers, designers and educators.

Crossing Boundaries. Ideas and Experiences in Dialogue for a New Culture of Education and Adults, Carlina Rinaldi (2006), edizioni junior, Reggio Children.
This book contains a collection of transcripts of presentations made by speakers from around the world at the Crossing Boundaries International Conference held in Reggio Emilia in February 2004. This was an important year, as it celebrated 40 years of the municipal preschools. The conference was dedicated to Loris Malaguzzi, the founding pedagogue of the Reggio Approach.

Dialogues with Places, Filippini, T., Giudici, C. and Vecchi, V. (eds) (2008), Reggio Children.
Children attending the infant–toddler centres and preschools in Reggio Emilia explored the Loris Malaguzzi Centre while it was a building site. This book is a big working notebook recording how the children chose a space they deemed to be interesting and planned a work, a gift for the selected place in the Centre.

Everyday Utopias (DVD) *– A Day in an Infant-Toddler Centre and a Day in a Preschool,* (2011), Reggio Children.
A perfect way to experience the Reggio Approach for yourself as you watch two examples of everyday practice in the infant–toddler centres and preschools of Reggio Emilia.

In Dialogue with Reggio Emilia: *Listening, Researching and Learning,* Carlina Rinaldi (2006), Routledge.
This book offers a selection of Carlina Rinaldi's most important articles, lectures and interviews from 1984 to 2006, with introductions explaining the context which inspired each piece. This is the first time much of the material has been published in English.

Making Learning Visible: Children as Individual and Group Learners, Giudici, C., Rinaldi, C. and Krechevsky, M. (eds) (2001), Reggio Children. A joint publication with Project Zero at Harvard University in the USA. This looks at the learning of children and adults in groups and gives very detailed examples of daily life in a preschool and infant–toddler centre. It is an ideal text for supporting continuous professional development.

Not Just Anyplace (video) (2003), Reggio Children.
This video tells the story of the Reggio experience from its earliest beginnings in Villa Cella. The philosophy and pedagogy are described by educators working in Reggio, and there are some short video sequences filmed in the preschools and infant–toddler centres.

One City, Many Children, Filippini, T., Giudici, C. and Vecchi, V. (eds) (2012), Reggio Children.
The story about the creation and the development of the preschools and infant–toddler centres in Reggio Emilia: a broad research project which joined together voices and thoughts of many different protagonists.

Reggio Tutta: A Guide to the City by the Children, Davoli, M. and Ferri, G. (eds) (2000), Reggio Children.
A description of a long-term project involving all the preschools and infant–toddler centres in Reggio Emilia. An example of the strong relationships that exist between the children of Reggio Emilia and the city itself.

REMIDA Day, Ferrari, A. and Giacopini, E. (eds) (2005), Reggio Children.
An account of the various events held around the city of Reggio Emilia to celebrate REMIDA day. The photographs are inspiring and certainly raise one's aspirations for what can be achieved with 'scrap' materials and 'junk'.

Theatre Curtain: The Ring of Transformations, Vecchi, V. (ed.) (2002), Reggio Children.
A beautifully illustrated description of the project carried out by children from the Diana School which led to the production of the safety curtain for the Ariosto Theatre. A detailed description of a long-term project.

The Hundred Languages of Children: Narrative of the Possible, Filippini, T. and Vecchi, V. (eds) (1997), Reggio Children.
The catalogue produced to accompany the 1996 version of *The Hundred Languages of Children* exhibition. Still relevant, it contains descriptions and essays which explain the context of many of the projects which formed part of the exhibition.

The Hundred Languages of Children: The Reggio Emilia Approach – Advanced Reflections (2nd edn), Edwards, C., Gandini, L. and Forman, G. (eds) (1998), Albex Publishing.
A collection of interviews with pedagogistas, atelieristas, teachers and administrators from Reggio Emilia, who describe their roles in their own words. This book also contains the transcript of an extended interview with Loris Malaguzzi in which he talks eloquently about the work of the preschools and infant–toddler centres, explaining why things are as they are. Essays and research papers from educators in the USA describe how they have been touched by the Reggio experience.

The Languages of Food – Recipes, Experiences, Thoughts, Cavallini, I. and Tedeschi, M. (eds) (2008), Reggio Children.
This book looks at the importance of the languages of food in the infant–toddler centres and preschools of Reggio Emilia. It includes not only healthy-eating guidelines, recipes and nutritional advice but illustrates the pedagogical value of food, meals and mealtimes. The book is exquisitely illustrated.

The Municipal Infant–Toddler Centres and Preschools of Reggio Emilia: Historical Notes and General Information (1999), Reggio Children.
A description of the organisation and management of the network of preschools and infant–toddler centres. A good source of factual information, although the statistical information is now out of date.

The Park is . . ., Cavallini, I., Filippini, T., Trancossi, L. and Vecchi, V. (eds) (2008), Reggio Children.
The first in a series, the Coriandoli series, which aims to capture a range of projects carried out in different preschools. The publications reflect the material put together directly by teachers, atelieristas and pedagogistas to share with parents and children in their own schools.

The Wonder of Learning, Cavallini, I., Filippini,T., Vecchi, V. and Trancossi L. (eds) (2011), *Browsing through Ideas*, Filipini, T. & Vecchi, V. (eds) (2009), *The Black Rubber Column*, Mennino, I. (ed.) (2009), Reggio Children.
This series reflects the content of the exhibition *The Wonder of Learning*. The three publications aim to deepen the projects displayed in the exhibition by documenting the children's learning processes and strategies.

Reggio Children publications are available in the UK from:

Sightlines Initiative
www.sightlines-initiative.com

Index